Heidi Rebekah Vegh

A Widow's Story from Loss to New Life

A Hard Journey to the Good

Copyright ® 2025 by Heidi Vegh
Published by UNITED HOUSE Publishing
All rights reserved. No portion of this book may be reproduced or shared in any form - electronic, printed, photocopied, recording, or by any information storage or retrieval system, without prior written permission from the publisher. The use of short quotations is permitted.

Scripture quotations taken from The Holy Bible, New International Version®, NIV®. Copyright © 1973, 1978, 1984, 2011 by Biblica, Inc. Used with permission of Zondervan.
All rights reserved worldwide. www.zondervan.com

ISBN - 978-1-952840-70-8

UNITED HOUSE Publishing Clarkston, Michigan
info@unitedhousepublishing.com www.unitedhousepublishing.com
Author Photograph: Chelsea Marie Imagery; chelsea.marie.imagery1@gmail.com

Photographer: Chelsea Smith, Chelsea Marie Imagery
chelsea.marie.imagery1@gmail.com

Interior Design: Talitha McGuinness; talitha@unitedhousepublishing.com
Printed in the United States of America 2025 - First Edition

SPECIAL SALES:
Most UNITED HOUSE books are available at special quantity discounts when purchased in bulk by corporations, organizations, and special interest groups. For more information, please email orders@unitedhousepublishing.com.

A Hard Journey to the Good

Dear Jesus, Thank you for showing up for me just as you promised you would. Thank you for pulling beauty out of ashes and giving me a firm ground to stand on, even in my darkest days. Thank you for guiding me out into the light of healing and blessing me with a beautiful new life where, even amid grief, you have proved your goodness.

A Hard Journey to the Good

Chapter 1
The One About Our Life

*Teach us to number our days, that we may gain
a heart of wisdom.*
Psalm 90:12

A Hard Journey to the Good

The air was cool, with a slight summer breeze squeezing through the closed blinds. I had forgotten who was on the schedule for chemo. My husband had several appointments that week, and keeping track of who was going with him each time turned into a part-time job.

"Who is going with me today?" Benji's crackling voice whispered. I crept to the calendar and saw that today was me. Benji needed a companion during his chemo sessions; he had gained debilitating anxiety after his cancer diagnosis and could no longer be alone. He needed someone to comfort him, distract him, pray with him, and be the buffer when the doctors sat down to explain the treatment or ask how he was doing.

His positive demeanor surprised the staff as he exaggerated how well he was doing. It was my job to gently reverse the vision of greatness and coat it with the slimy reality that chemo was taking him apart, bit by tiny bit. There always has to be a realist in these scenarios, and I was given the grueling task of keeping the oncologist connected to reality. I longed to be optimistic and hopeful that this prognosis of imminent death would be proven wrong, that God was going to heal him this side of heaven. My faith struggled as I faced the daily reality that Benji would most likely be leaving me for a bigger and better place, leaving me to cope as an only parent on this cold, dark Earth to carry grief and sorrow too heavy for me to hold. I knew it would crush me, relentlessly waiting for me to give up breathing, give up living, and give up hope.

Almost overnight, I had become a thirty-something makeshift nurse, running on fumes and the occasional shower. Benji was a shell of his former self. I didn't recognize the couple reflecting at us through the dresser mirror as we stood together, taking in what we had become. The thin, white, and washed-out man standing next to me was a foreigner in my life. The vibrant, hilarious, and adventure-seeking man whom I married had vanished, leaving me behind to wallow in the service of a rapidly aging, thirty-three-year-old technology director. His flesh and blood remained, but I could not recognize him through the cold, sheer skin that now cradled his small, frail body.

My husband disappeared in front of my eyes, and I went with him. I am a frail woman by nature, but grief and trauma had torn at my flesh, leaving what was only needed. Bones, muscle, and a pumping heart. If I had control of my breathing, I may have chosen not to continue.

Years before cancer disrupted our lives, if I were to be asked what I took delight in, it would be travel, exploring the world, and seasoning my knowledge of it with its breathtaking God-given beauty and diverse and colorful cultures.

We owned a small house in a cramped lot near downtown Salt Lake City. We had a pocket-sized patch of grass in the backyard. Before we had babies and toddlers demanding our attention, we would lay a blanket under the stars and drift into daydream land, expressing our desires for an adventurous life.

In his final days, those desires fell off him like scales, and his only contentment was in this house, on this plot of land, in this city. He knew this place would be his final resting place, far beyond my naive daydreaming.

I would have jumped at an opportunity to live in other states, cities, or countries. I deposited these notions in his mind over our many years together, but something always called him to stay put, to be content and comfortable. Many years later, I would finally understand why his determination to stay was the best possible thing for us, for me.

We lived in Utah, a vast landscape of differing scenery with mountains, lakes, and the scorching, red rock deserts of the south. In the spring of 2012, his health had taken an upturn in his ten-year battle with Crohn's disease. We found ourselves soaking in the warm desert air and waking up next to our young boys in the "Taj Mahal" of tents, resting in the picturesque Zion National Park. Our friends made fun of us for purchasing the monstrosity of a tent at Costco earlier that year. Still, we loved it. It had three "rooms" with plenty of space for all the camping necessities. We had one of those gigantic blowup mattresses that stood taller than a regular bed. We were in nature's luxury.

A Hard Journey to the Good

When we woke each morning and fixed our eyes on the tent screen above us, we witnessed the glorious sheer red rock cliff with the reflection of the newly risen sunshine glowing it awake. Our boys were nestled just below our view in their soft, footed pajamas, eyes barely open, awaiting a new and mysterious day. We eagerly rode the tram up to the mountain hikes. The boys were busy with anticipation as their little legs hung over the bench seats, dangling and kicking with excitement. We parked and walked a short distance to Weeping Rock, a red rock that appears to be weeping with millions of tiny waterfalls rushing down into the damp soil. Perhaps it was crying for us that day. Perhaps it knew something we didn't.

We both crouched to snap a photo of the four of us, Jonah in my arms and Isaac in Benji's. We all smiled at the camera, unknowingly snapping one of the final photos we would take of our healthy life and one that would take residence on a GoFundMe page only months later. GoFundMe pages held pictures of other people, foreign suffering, and people trudging through life-altering trials. It wasn't for the four of us. But it would be.

Months later, we were resorting to dark bedrooms, half-drank glasses of water, and anti-anxiety pills. I longed for the old days. I longed for the old life. I festered with the statistics of losing a spouse at age thirty-three. How did I get so unlucky? But at the same time, I was the luckiest girl in the world to have had such a brilliant and loving husband to do life with. Cut short, perhaps, but lucky.

I heard Benji shift in bed with a little moan, and I walked in and found him sitting up. A rare sight in those days.

His breathless voice whimpered, "More water, more pills."

"I'll get them for you, honey," I whispered.

This is what we had become.

We met when we were sixteen. I had transferred to a private Christian school because I was utterly lost in the public school system; my grades were horrific, and the only way out was to change everything. It was a risky move for my parents, but I trusted they were making the right decision for me.

I was welcomed with open arms into the small Christian community. I tried out for cheer and made the team. The opportunities were less competitive, and I was thrilled to start my junior year with such a valuable place. There was a boy. Cute, popular, funny. We became friends and hit it off. I had heard of Benji. My best friend, Andrea, had a crush on him long before I arrived, and I knew he was off-limits. However, my heart couldn't lie, so we started dating.

My friendship with Andrea was damaged, but years later, we reconciled and are still friends today.

Benji and I were surrounded by faith-filled people in our school. We lived our lives reliant on God, spending our weekends at youth events and our summers at church camp. We blasted DC TALK and The Newsboys in our small hatchback cars and encouraged each other as we lived out our faith.

God was real to both of us. Our childhoods were deeply contrasted. His was more traumatic and challenging with divorced parents, and mine was more traditional with parents who loved each other and did their best to raise us to know God. These childhood experiences served us well as we strived to live for Jesus.

Our faith grew us together, and we held strong convictions to wait until marriage to be intimate. Our relationship was pure, innocent, and based on our love for each other and our love for God.

We spent our junior and senior years together. Moving faster than any of our parents felt comfortable with, we were engaged eighteen months after graduation.

We were married on September 15, 2000. I woke up that clear morning eager to marry my best friend. The last six months of planning were finally coming to fruition, and I could not believe the day had finally arrived. I spent the morning with my precious sisters and friends, dolling up, laughing, and relishing in the beauty of the late summer day.

We got married at a historical building in Salt Lake City called the Old Meeting House. It was large and formal, with sage green and pink hues showered throughout. The wedding colors I chose resembled the colors of the venue.

As the ceremony began, I took my New Vogue roses and held them tightly to my chest; my dad took my hand, noticeably shaking, and walked me around the corner. Tears fell, and my lips trembled as I walked slowly down the aisle. I approached Benji as he welcomed me onto the stage. The moment had arrived—the moment we had anticipated for several years. We were finally going to be husband and wife. We glided through the ceremony, witnessed by the people who cherished us most. We promised to love each other fully, to walk in forgiveness and grace. We promised to keep God at the center of our marriage, and we promised to be together until death parts us, the stingy reality of that looming in our unknown future.

The reception was swarming with friends and relatives. The cake was cut, the dancing took over, and when the celebration ended, we danced through a tunnel of bubbles, escaping the wedding chaos in our brand-new Ford Focus, off on an adventure we could not have anticipated would end so soon.

Looking back, I can see the hand of the Lord weaving His plan into my life. He directed my steps and led me to my husband. Nothing is wasted when it is ordained by the Lord. God knew we would only have thirteen years together. He knew that one day, September 15th, would hold a sense of bitterness and loss as I struggled to celebrate. Wedding anniversaries for a left-behind spouse are days that just simply should not exist. What should I say? Who do I call? What do I think? Saying "Happy Anniversary" without a response always leaves me feeling abandoned and angry.

So often, when we think of life's heavy loads and agonizing losses, we either turn to God for comfort or turn away in anger. We can't fathom that a loving God would allow for seemingly senseless loss. We struggle to believe the deep and true character of God is good when we don't see goodness in our circumstances. Jesus never promised we would live a trouble-free life; He only promised He would be with us through the troubles (John 16:33).

Benji was diagnosed with Crohn's disease the day before our engagement in February 2000. I had anticipated our engagement for many months, and although I knew what was coming, he planned an extravagant night. We traveled the city in a sleek back limo, shared a meal at Christopher's Steak House, and parked at a lookout point with a starry night view of stunning Salt Lake City. He gently led me out of the limo onto a spot of grass-covered land and got down on one knee. The limo driver snapped a photo that has long since disappeared into the abyss of developed photos lodged somewhere in the dusty attic. Although I was not surprised, my small hand shook as I held it out for him to slip on the platinum diamond ring, the first lavish item I ever owned. It was too big and slipped around on my narrow ring finger. I sat in the limo, holding it in place as I snuggled my fiance with tears of joy streaming down my young face.

The next day would prove to be in deep contrast. We didn't have cell phones then, so our daytime conversations were from a slimy payphone in the lunchroom of my office. I stood there, phone clenched in my hand. Benji said straightforwardly, "The results came back and said I have something called Crohn's disease. I don't even know what that means."

"Wow. I don't either. We will figure this out," I told him with hope in my voice.

This would begin a long journey of learning and striving for answers and healing.

The doctors were unschooled in this disease and only simply prescribed steroids to control the inflammation of the colon, where the disease lived. There was no talk of changing his diet or lifestyle, simply drugs. This did not sit well with us or our family. Steroids are dangerous and life-altering in terms of side effects. We were determined to seek out alternative treatment when we came upon a special diet called SCD (specific carbohydrate diet). It is specific to vegetable carbohydrates and meat, grain-free, and low in sugar. The resources were limited, but we were able to get our hands on several cookbooks that helped us walk through this challenging lifestyle. We had our times of healing and rejuvenation when the diet was working, and he was in rhythm with the obscure way of living and eating. We had our challenging times when the hearty burgers and fries at the local pub got the best of him, plunging him to the bathroom in agony and defeat. This was a strenuous journey full of hills and valleys. We walked through this harrowing road for many years, waiting for healing that would never come on Earth.

In 2004, we purchased our first house after several years of apartment hopping through the Salt Lake Valley. Our life was like a floating feather as we drifted here and there, following our friends and experiencing life in the city. We both grew up in church and became Jesus' followers at a very young age. We knew God and loved God, but we had allowed Him to drift from the center of our lives.

We spent our weekends drinking at dance clubs and having parties that kept our neighbors up. I still have the same Bible where I wrote notes about that time of our life. God was in my heart and mind; He was with me in the quiet of the night when I stayed up late reading the Psalms, but we sadly didn't include him in our weekend escapades. I was unsure how to marry the two lifestyles. I felt torn in my spirit and as a couple, but I didn't know how to get us back onto a road following Jesus.

We moved into our first home on a crisp, cool October day. My mom made a large pot of pulled pork sandwiches for our weary, box-lifting friends, and we were proud of the accomplishment of owning property in the snug and hip neighborhood of Sugarhouse. The trees lined the narrow roads, enveloping antique homes with wraparound porches. Our house was old and musty but had a bit of charm. Our apartment-sized furniture barely filled the rooms as we hosted our friends and watched as the space became the epicenter of gatherings, barbeques, holiday celebrations, and birthday parties. Our hearts were in the hosting.

This was all the while piling up to be one of the most difficult parts of losing my Benji. He was warped into the walls, the long conversations near the fireplace, the smell of freshly brewed hops wafting into the windows on a warm summer day. This was his place—his sanctuary, our sanctuary.

We worked hard to make it our own. In the early days of homeownership, we decided to paint one of the upstairs bedrooms but had never done such a thing. My parents came over to give us tips and how-tos on trimming it out first and rolling at an angle. The room took hours upon hours to paint, but we finally had a finished product.

Years later, I have painted countless walls in my homes, and I always think back to that experience and cherish everything we learned together.

We spent our time working, going to school, and updating the house. We loved to travel and spent any extra money we had on trips. We traveled the country, visiting friends and family, exploring new places, and coming home with knick-knacks to place around our home. I would purchase a frame from each city we were visiting, fill it with a printed picture of us, and place it on a shelf in our basement. Soon, the shelf became full. Full of us. Full of our adventures. A friend of ours called it a shrine of our experiences. These same pictures would one day be lined up in the funeral home in Millcreek, honoring those distant times.

Our favorite place to visit was the Pacific Northwest. Benji's grandparents lived in British Columbia, a little town just over the border called Hope. We would often fly to Seattle, rent a car, and make the four-hour drive north to the small, quaint community. We explored that small corner of Canada, including Vancouver, and when we headed back to Seattle, we often found ourselves doing all the touristy things. I have family in that part of the state as well, so we would make plans to spend time with them.

One day, nearing the end of one of our trips, we stopped at a brewery as we headed south towards the airport. We wove through the tree-lined streets, and I commented we could find happiness in this corner of the world. There were many technology job opportunities in Seattle, and I thought if God were to ever take us out of Utah, that is where I would want to live. I had a heart for adventure and would have loved to move to other cities we visited, like Boston or Austin, but the Seattle area somehow felt like home.

I often struggled with confidence when it came to choosing a career path. In contrast, Benji was the opposite—focused, driven, and able to envision a successful future in technology long before I even entered the picture. I envied his vision and his drive. I wandered. I stuck my toe in many fields as I trudged my way through general and elective courses at the local community college. Once I received my Associate's Degree, I spent a small stint at the University of Utah, studying English with aspirations of being a high school English teacher. That fell flat, and in 2005, I decided to jump head-first into cosmetology school, another twist in the long tale of Heidi trying to figure out what she wanted to be when she grew up.

I was striving to graduate on time, and at this point, I had dreams of a long, successful career working in a salon. After an exhausting year, I graduated in January 2006 with my cosmetology license and was thankful to finally have school behind me.

While we were still in high school, Benji's passion for technology landed him his first job as a graveyard shift tech support agent. He answered tech support calls in a dark, quiet office. I would often visit him after my shift at the shoe store across the street in the mall.

After paying his dues, Benji landed a well-paying job as the technology manager at a local insurance company, which was just one of the stepping stones to an eventual stellar career. Although he never attended college, Benji obtained a long list of certifications and experience that equaled much more than a degree. This proved to be one of his biggest losses when he became sick. He lost his ability to focus. He felt uncomfortable being at the office because of his need for frequent bathroom trips. Facing the slow and steady loss of his ability to engage in his passion devastated him to his core.

One cold night in early January, shortly after my graduation from cosmetology school, we were sitting around the table at Chili's with our best friends Scott and Kami, and I mentioned I was five days late for my cycle. Kami's excitement burst as she planned to pick up a pregnancy test for me on the way to our house later. Benji and I stood in our tiny, tiled bathroom, staring at the stick as our friends impatiently waited downstairs. It was positive—a baby.

We jumped, laughed, and cried with our friends as we all tried to wrap our heads around this new knowledge. We had been planning a trip to Europe later that year, so I said, "Time to put the Europe book away and get out the baby book." Benji's look was one of stunned, pure excitement. There was no going back now. The trip to Europe would not happen for sixteen years, amazingly enough, with the same friends, but without Benji.

Shortly after our big news, I was offered a job at a local Aveda salon. I had dreamed of working for Aveda for many years and was thrilled to be able to offer my services to such a beautiful company. My pregnancy was, for the most part, uneventful, except for the ER run after a fall and unknown pressure during the last weeks. Benji was so supportive and never became anxious. He held me and supported me in all my worst new-mom fears. He assured me Jonah would be perfect and healthy and would arrive at the perfect time.

On September 6, 2006, we went in for a routine check-up and learned the fluid surrounding the baby was low. They recommended an induction two days later. I was filled with uncertainty. We had worked so hard planning for a natural birth with hypnobirthing. We practiced meditation, breathing, and visualizing. We were as ready as we would ever be to bring this baby into the world as naturally as possible. I didn't want drugs, and I didn't want to feel like a sick person in the hospital. I knew God created my body to endure childbirth, and I was determined to feel everything and experience the birth of my child as fully as I could.

This diagnosis of low fluid shifted our plans. On the morning of September 8th, we were packed and ready to go, just waiting for the hospital to call and let us know they had room for us. We sat at the kitchen table, watching The Office to pass the time, as I spun my hips on the birthing ball, eating scrambled eggs. I was ready for this. He was ready for this.

Once in the hospital, Pitocin was injected, and it was time to wait: wait for a slow progression of labor and the intense, induced contractions that would follow. Our room was filled with soft music, lavender oils, and a quiet, calming peace. I was an anomaly in the labor and delivery department, as they did not often have women who declined an epidural. I was a spectacle, and they were shocked when they could see I was enduring the pain without help.

Benji never left my side; he calmed, held, and encouraged me. Our doula guided my movement and positions.

After nearly twelve hours and an eventual unwanted epidural, Jonah Benjamin made his dramatic appearance in the world, complete with a wound on his head from the suction cup. But he was perfect.

We were parents. We were no longer a couple but a family. We had Jonah in our arms, healthy and perfect. Benji was ecstatic as he shared pictures of him with our closest friends and family. I was euphoric. The peace that overcame me as I held my baby was intoxicating . . . until it wasn't.

We arrived home with Jonah, and the following weeks proved to be some of the darkest of my life. I suffered from intense postpartum depression that nearly took me out. It became severe enough to talk to my doctor, and she encouraged me to seek a counselor. I never did. I endured alone. I suffered alone in my dark thoughts. I had thoughts of hurting Jonah that petrified me. I felt anxious for the first time in my life, and when evening came and the night crawled closer, I began to panic inside, unsure of what the night would hold.

I wasn't prepared for the emotional intensity I would experience as a first-time mom. I didn't understand, and I didn't know who to talk to. Over time, it did pass, but it would leave me traumatized and fearful of its return. Jonah was an angel baby—he rarely cried. He slept, ate, and played on cue. He was the calm in my storm.

When Jonah was ten months old, we got another surprise. Our son Isaac was on his way. He proved to be the opposite of our sweet, calm, and easy Jonah. The name Isaac means "laughter," so we knew we were in for a treat.

Isaac's labor was much the same. It was intense and dramatic and ended with unwanted pain meds. Isaac came out loud, silly, and eccentric. He cried for the first five months of his life. He climbed out of his crib and would never take a nap. He spent his time creating messes and making us laugh until we cried. The postpartum depression did try to rear its ugly head one evening while I nursed and rocked my infant in the corner of our small, dimly lit room. I knew that if I succumbed to the fear and anxiety that so begrudgingly wanted to take root inside of me, I would not have been able to climb out.

I laid Isaac on the bed, and I knelt. I addressed the enemy, raising my voice at the fear. I rebuked the attack on my mind and refused, with all my might, to allow this evil to penetrate my soul. I defeated the enemy that night by the power of the Holy Spirit and the mighty name of Jesus. Those spirits of depression, anxiety, and dark thoughts never returned.

Jonah and Isaac balance each other out, and I can see they make a perfect little Benji together. God knew I would need to see Benji still walking on this Earth years later. Jonah has his mind, and Isaac has his face.

I catch myself looking at my boys in awe. I notice the shapes of their noses, the parts in their hair, and the movements of their hands. I see Benji living and breathing through them. I hear Benji in their cracking voices. Jonah is now the same age as Benji was when I met him. My heart rattles in despair when Jonah talks about his passion for technology and space. It's as though Benji's passions transferred directly into Jonah's heart and mind.

A Hard Journey to the Good

The years of two babies under two wore me down. It brought a level of exhaustion that pulled at my body and siphoned any logical sense out of my mind. These were days of sleep deprivation that forced us to doubt our capacity to have more children. After Jonah was born, we began to attend church again. We attended once in our childless years but had trouble connecting or finding any sense of belonging. Being a mother forced connection to other women and helped me see firsthand that I was not alone. Shortly after Isaac was born, our church started a MOPS group. I had a new passion develop inside of me to serve, to be a part of something bigger than me, and to gain authentic friendships that went past pleasantries.

I sat at the table at our first MOPS (Mothers of Preschoolers) meeting. Jonah was with the other toddlers, and Isaac was nursing in my arms. I was stretched thin and barely had the mental capacity to gather anything meaningful into my consciousness. Over the months and years at MOPS, I developed a passion for leadership and serving. I led tables and eventually led the entire group. I began to come into my own in the body of Christ.

Benji supported me, but being a part of Jesus' working family didn't fuel him. He attended church with me and shook the hands of my friends' husbands, but it rarely gained more depth. I was solo at many events as he was often working or busy brewing beer on a frozen Sunday morning. Benji was a man of passion. His beer won awards, well, the accolades of all his friends, at least. He would set up a brewery on our flagstone patio on a bitter winter morning. The large stainless steel pot steamed with the fresh hops he had meticulously picked out at the local brewing store. He learned by doing. He gained understanding and knowledge; he tried and failed. If the beer were green or flat, he would try again. He purchased a kegerator and installed it in our basement. He had custom taps with signs labeling the names of his creations. He named one after me. He often called me "feisty," so he named the beer "hefefiesten." The sign hung over the taps with fishing line, and he often led our visitors downstairs to taste his delicious brew named after his first and only love.

Years later, as I scrolled his phone, I would find photos of myself—photos I didn't realize he was taking—photos of me cooking or getting ready, photos of the boys and me, photos of me walking or talking to friends, and close-up pictures as if he needed to savor each moment he had with me. Finding them years later sent my heart sinking.

Benji loved people. He loved all people no matter who they were, where they came from, or what they had done. I was always hearing about new people he met. He was intimately interested in their life stories and what they were about. He didn't hesitate to invite people over at the last minute. He often walked through the door after work, trailed by a new friend. It would take me off guard as I was never prepared for company. I was self-conscious about the state of our home or whether we had enough food to go around. He never wanted anyone to feel left out, and he couldn't stand if someone didn't have a place to go for a holiday meal. He loved hosting parties and get-togethers for any reason and for anything worth celebrating.

Before our boys arrived, our home was often filled with friends of all types: work friends, church friends, and high school friends. They would mingle and befriend each other. Many people developed lifelong friendships because of their association with Benji. He was a gatherer. I never was. I liked people, but he brought out the hostess in me.
He had a passion for life. He had a desire to make the best out of every circumstance. I believed he sensed his time on this planet would be fleeting.

Chapter 2
The One Where It Started to Hurt

*"God knows our situation;
He will not judge us as if we had no difficulties to
overcome. What matters is the sincerity and
perseverance of our will to overcome them."*
C.S. Lewis[1]

A Hard Journey to the Good

We could feel the warm ocean air glide into our little room on the Royal Caribbean ship that had been circling the Gulf of Mexico for the last few days. We were on a cruise with our best friends, without our kids, exploring, laughing, and creating memories—memories that would prove to be the last of their kind. Our friends and I didn't know that one year later, we wouldn't be sipping Mai Tais on a beach in Honduras; we would be gathering in shock, utter despair, and utter loss, drinking for different reasons. Not to celebrate but to numb.

Benji said that sunny afternoon in our stateroom, "I have a strange pain in my abdomen. I'm sure it's just because I have been working out, or maybe I ate something weird. I'm sure it's nothing." He was always one to quickly push it aside and blame it on something like food, stress, or an injury. He was petrified his Crohn's disease could be taking a turn for the worse. "I'm sure it's nothing," I assured him. However, deep inside, I also felt something was wrong. He had a strange sore on his leg, and over the last summer, he had suffered from odd infections in his mouth and throat. I had the sense his body was filled with infection or something worse.

One night, a few months earlier, he awoke from a frightening dream, causing him to jolt out of bed, trip, and break his finger. We sat on the couch in the middle of the night, pondering at the oddity of the situation. This injury led to him retreating from his daily workouts, possibly what was keeping his Crohn's disease at bay and sending him into a spiral of sickness and infection. Unbeknownst to us, that was the beginning of our tragedy. I often wonder what he dreamed that night. Perhaps it was a foreshadowing of what was to come. Maybe he knew.

At that moment, in the cruise ship cabin, I stuffed the fear, got dressed, and met our friends for dinner. We had a life to live. We couldn't allow the unknown to take away from our joyful experiences. We were young, traveling, kid-less, and free. We didn't want to let anything hold us down. We agreed when we returned home, he would see a doctor, but until then, we would make the most of this trip. It was the last true vacation we would ever take together.

We arrived home from the Caribbean in early October. Benji made an appointment with his naturopath to get his strange symptoms hopefully explained. The doctor ordered an ultrasound, as he suspected he had a hernia, but we never received clear answers.

The boys and I would often meet Benji for lunch near his work. One particular day, Jonah was in kindergarten, so I just had little Isaac with me. Isaac had gotten out of school earlier since he was only in preschool. We drove twenty minutes to a local burger shop. We ordered our food and sat in deep conversation as Isaac scarfed down his order of fries. His precious ears could hear the words spoken but were not mature enough to understand the gravity.

We sat with our burgers and our littlest man, and Benji asked in frustration, "Why don't we have answers yet? Maybe we should make an appointment with a regular doctor."

I agreed. Perhaps moving from a naturopath and moving down a more traditional route was what we needed to do to get the answers we needed.

We had always lived holistically. We didn't want a doctor who was only interested in prescribing the latest and greatest drug with its laundry list of side effects. We wanted holistic guidance that was more centered around lifestyle and healthy living. However, at this point, we were at the end of our patience and realized we should perhaps relinquish our ideals and see a regular doctor.

As the end of October approached, his pain became increasingly worse, and we decided to visit the ER. We found childcare and made our way up the winding roads to the University of Utah hospital, nestled in the foothills of the Wasatch Mountains. When we arrived, they were quick to get us in, and after triage, they decided it was best to get an MRI to see if they could find a cause for his suffering. He laid back on the gurney as his anxieties rose with every minute of the wait. Hospitals made Benji nervous. He had never spent much time in one, and he was shrouded in the fear of sickness and death. He felt that if he ever ended up in the hospital, his worst nightmares were coming to life. Perhaps, now, they were.

We sat in silence and could hear the whimperings of other patients and the calming whispers of the nurses. He lay there, still, almost numb with fear at what we would learn.

The doctor slid back the curtain and stood at the end of the bed. "Benji, we have found three small abscesses in your abdomen. These are pockets of infection that need to be drained immediately." He slithered back out the curtain, leaving us stunned and confused.

Benji was immediately admitted.

They wheeled him down the hall into a room with an MRI machine that he laid underneath while they inserted tubes into his abdomen to allow for drainage of the toxic fluid. Benji writhed in pain as each one was inserted, one of them being between his ribs. My gut wrenched tightly, listening to his small wails as I gently caressed his fingers. He had the smoothest skin between his knuckles, and as I rubbed the soft skin, I whispered prayers of strength for my suffering husband.

We spent two long nights in the hospital, and in an abrupt and surprising turn of events, they discharged us much earlier than expected. The nurse stood staunchly as I muttered concern for him through tears. I envisioned the weight I would inevitably carry as we were left to ourselves at home without a constant watch. They trained me to measure the fluid and record the amount that was being released into the clear tubes into plastic cups. I set up a makeshift nurse's station next to our bed, and for the next few days, I embraced my new role and added a caregiver to my title, which was right under wife and mother. I still felt desperately unequipped for this new job.

His nightstand was no longer a place for a warm cup of coffee and his latest novel. It now stored gauze, tape, measuring cups, gloves, and water—the first physical shift from normal.

The days following the release from the hospital were desperate, but beautiful. As I cared for Benji in a different capacity than merely a wife, it became clear that our roles were turning. From this point on, our level of intimacy was gradually fading. The deviation from lover to caretaker slowly started to take form. Our bedroom turned from a place of intimacy to a place of survival. The smells turned to one of sterile surgery as I had to learn to measure bodily fluid. I had to learn to share my concerns in ways that wouldn't alarm him or make him feel inadequate as a husband. We needed to maintain a delicate balance to avoid resentment or embarrassment.

The boys were often confused and retaliated with misbehavior or tantrums. Their innocence was slowly and agonizingly being stripped from their precious souls.

As days turned into weeks, and after several trips back to the hospital to remove or replace tubes, we found ourselves back in the ER with his unbearable pain. This time, we were taken more seriously, and the doctors were truly caving to the idea that something else was happening. Something unusual and something around which they could barely wrap their educated minds. They admitted him once again.

I tore myself from my solo bed every morning to head back to the hospital. I was overcome by the logistics of the boys getting to and from two different schools, pick-ups, car seats, meals, and bedtimes. All normal routines turned haywire in our new lifestyle of hospital living. I chose to sleep at home each night as I didn't want to interrupt the small rhythms the boys were used to. But each day, I was back up to Benji, waiting for doctors, tests, and results.

Although we had grown up knowing the love of Jesus, Benji had demons to fight. He was traumatized by a tumultuous childhood and struggled with the reality that a loving God would allow bad things to happen. He was fascinated with space and all things science. He researched the complexities of space and the vastness of the universe. He wished, in a different life, he had become an astronaut but knew that his failing body would never have allowed him to pursue that dream. His faith in God wavered, and he questioned the validity of the Bible. I know he experienced God's truth in his heart, and my desires to teach our boys about the love of God were never questioned. But He needed proof. He needed tangible evidence. His understanding, or lack of understanding, of suffering left him confused and disillusioned by a supposed all-loving God.

One afternoon, I returned home to tend to the boys, and our pastor, Troy, spent some time talking with Benji in the hospital room. Benji met God that day. He described a miraculous encounter with our great and loving God. He described peace despite his dire circumstances and was determined to tell everyone about this grand experience in that hospital bed.

From then on, his faith was evident in thought, word, and deed. He still struggled with intense anxiety, but he now knew where to take it. He took it to the feet of Jesus. He relied on the medication when needed, but he experienced God in such a real and raw way—he simply transformed in front of my eyes.

Our time in the hospital felt futile, and the conclusions were anticlimactic. They were able to get the infections under control, but recommended Benji receive a colonoscopy for further testing. We made the appointment for the end of January, a brutal month away, and were released just before Christmas. We left the hospital after one full week and headed home to wait.

As I packed up a week's worth of hospital life, he stood at the window and took in the beautiful Salt Lake Valley view with gratitude. He was thankful for the life-changing experience. I snapped a photo of the intimate contemplation of his experience. He intentionally took in this experience. He didn't want to walk out of that hospital unchanged. He didn't want it to be for nothing. He wanted to gain something from each of his experiences and feel it as deeply as possible, with a rooted longing to share what God had done in his life. We arrived home and spent Christmas with our sweet boys and family. The January colonoscopy loomed.

Although Benji was released from the hospital infection-free, the doctors were still perplexed by what was happening inside his body. He was still sick, still lacked energy, and still worried about Crohn's disease.

In the first week of 2013, the flu hit our home as if we needed more sickness, isolation, or suffering. All four of us had a cough and fever, and as my birthday approached, I was just well enough to celebrate. Benji placed a high value on celebrating, and my birthday was at the top of his list.

This year was different. He didn't feel well, and he didn't feel like planning or celebrating. I was turning thirty-three, an age defining the rest of my life.

I spent my birthday snowboarding with girlfriends and ended the day with a small group of dear friends at my home, eating take-out from Olive Garden and spending time together. Benji was asleep in the other room as we ate and giggled, and they showered me with love and gifts. I was blessed and honored to be celebrated, but my husband was missing. This experience foreshadowed what my life was to become—living life solo.

On January 29th, the dreaded colonoscopy arrived. It was a snowy Tuesday morning, and Benji, Isaac, and I drove to a hospital located west of our home. We were meandering our way through blizzardy snow that stuck to the ground, muffling out all sounds except for the large snow plow barreling down the road. We spent most of our drive in silence but were hopeful. We envisioned our future that day. We envisioned the medical professionals relaying that Crohn's disease was alive and well, but they knew exactly how to treat it. The medication would ease his symptoms, and he could continue to live a normal and vibrant life. We had visions of more travel, adventures, and experiences with our boys. As I drove through the blizzard, Benji sat hunched over in the seat next to me. He said quietly, "If I beat this thing, we should have another baby."

I reached over and grabbed his hand. "I hope so. I hope so."

We were abounding in hope at the future we had curated in our minds.

Benji was wheeled away from Isaac and me as we sat in a curtained area, impatiently awaiting the completion of the test and the much-anticipated results. Isaac jumped on and off the fabric chair as I tried to corral him from climbing on anything more dangerous. Isaac has always loved adventure, and a room filled with mysterious contraptions and climbing opportunities was right up his alley. His innocence melted off of him as these experiences became more commonplace in his fragile little life.

Within an hour, Benji was wheeled back in, groggy but responsive. They briefly let us be, so he could fully awake before discussing the results.

I sat next to the hospital bed as the doctor again pulled back the curtain, results in hand. The doctor muttered our worst fear. "We were unable to insert the probe correctly because there is a large tumor blocking his colon."

They did not tell us things looked normal for Crohn's disease. They did not tell us they had a medication that would give him a good life. Instead, the words "possible cancer" slithered out of the doctor's mouth like venom on a mission to poison every possible hope and dream we had for our future.

The shock was so intense it was as if I had run straight into a brick wall at break-neck speed. I looked at Benji, and he looked at me. We were in this together, and although his worst nightmare had become a reality, we held hands and vowed to keep going. We would wait for the biopsy results and take them as they came.

The next day, the kids were at school, and we had the house to ourselves. It was quiet. Our minds were spinning, but nothing was said. Benji's fast fingers were wrapped up in googling the possibility of a tumor being cancerous and what the chances were of getting cancer with Crohn's disease. All the answers stripped us of any hope of cancer not becoming part of our young lives.

I was downstairs when the text came through. The doctor sent a text.

"Small-cell cancer found in the tumor. The treatment is

chemotherapy. No surgery needed at this point." He yelled for me to join him upstairs. I sat next to him, white-faced in disbelief.

We had arrived. Benji was a cancer patient.

Benji shook, jolted up, and began pacing the room, his heart beating fast, his fears bubbling over, and his future of healing being stripped away.

I grabbed my phone and called my dear friend Tara. We needed someone else in the house, a sounding board, and another presence to dispel the gravitational force of emotion pulling us into a vortex of panic.

Tara arrived moments later just to be there—to listen, to encourage. She said, "This is when we tie a knot in our faith and hold on for dear life." I have had this mantra in my life since.

We were tying the knot; our fingers were bleeding. We were hanging on for Benji's life. We began to make the rounds of calls to close friends and family, and each time the word cancer escaped our lips, the reality sank deeper into our hearts. Our lives had made an unexpected turn. We had begun to wander down a dark path, covered in vines of uncertainty and potholes of the unknown.

Benji was riddled with anxiety as he paced the room. I was managing the anti-anxiety medication every few hours to keep it at a decent level. Our reality was coming unhinged, and we were hanging by a thread. Jesus served as our only lifeline.

We met with the oncologist, Dr. Floyd, the following day, and as we sat in the dimly lit room with the metal blinds hiding the January daylight outside, he explained the chemotherapy process. He told us where it would be administered and what it would feel like. We were given a stringy list of possible side effects and learned that blood draws and white blood cell counts would become part of our daily routine. Benji was already sick going into this, so they were monitoring his body with a careful eye. They knew he was weak, and chemotherapy was intense. Chemotherapy, essentially, has the sole purpose of killing everything in the body, including cancer. After the cancer is eradicated, the patient can begin to rebuild the destruction that took place. The unfortunate case for

Benji was that his body was already in decline.

But we hoped. We hoped this chemotherapy treatment would abolish the malicious cancer. Our minds dwelled on the doctors in the hospital who did not pick up on this only a month earlier. We felt disenchanted with the care of the doctors, yet we were now thrust into the hands of an oncologist who was supposed to know exactly what to do.

We learned that small-cell cancer is typically found in the lungs, so for it to be located in tumors throughout his abdomen was almost unheard of. When we spent our time Googling, there were only hints of studies done on this type of cancer, and each prognosis and outcome left us with little to no hope. But this simply could not be. This could not be our reality. We felt as though something was standing between our two souls, pushing us apart. Something didn't want us together anymore. Our family was facing destruction.

Dr. Floyd explained he needed a PET scan the next day to show how far the cancer had grown and spread. We were told the results would take a few days.

In the meantime, they ordered four rounds of chemotherapy for three days every three weeks. After the third round, they would do another scan to see the progress. After the traumatic appointment, we returned to Benji's sister's house and saturated ourselves in the love of family. We sat with his mom, his siblings, and their families. Later, my family came over to sit with us in the aftermath of the bombshell that had just exploded in our lives. We sat, we cried, and we were in shock.

In our distress, we all decided that a weekend at Disneyland was the next best thing to do. We knew that after chemotherapy started, it would be the entire focus of our lives, so we needed time away to connect and prepare for the long journey ahead. Although Benji was less than himself, he was willing to go and make the most of it.

Benji had his PET scan Thursday morning, and we were on a plane at 6 p.m. Being in the flaming depths of despair while simultaneously being in the happiest place on earth was a hard tension to live in, but we did our best for the sake of our small boys. Benji walked through the park the first morning, but I took him back to the room after lunch. He soaked in the tub and held tightly to his God.

Once he settled in the room, I returned to California Adventure, where the family was having lunch. I excused myself to the bathroom, and right there, next to the hand dryer, a flood of bottled-up emotion came spilling out, drowning everyone around me. Benji's sisters and Stepmom cried with me as I came to the full realization of what we were facing. I was facing a possible life without my love, and reality had set up camp in my soul.

We were all dreading the trip back to Salt Lake, especially Benji. We wanted to prolong any sort of normalcy, so we decided to stay one more day and spend time at the beach. We snagged a hip little room overlooking the ocean. We made s'mores by the beach fire and hashed out all the possible scenarios of our reality.

During our time in California, we learned cancer had spread to his colon, liver, and some lymph nodes around his pancreas, but the plan was the same.

He had his first treatment on Wednesday, February 6th. It was a simple IV. The medication flowing into my husband looked harmless, but we knew it was on a deadly mission. He went to treatment for three days, and the next week, he went in to test his NADIR (testing the white blood cell counts and platelets). The report was good. He felt like Ironman at that point, and although his energy was low, he would go on a long walk after his treatments, trying to feel like anything other than a cancer patient. Three weeks later, he had another treatment, and his blood started to lose the qualities of a healthy person. Blood cell counts started dropping, and we could now see the devastating effects of chemotherapy on the human body. The Ironman complex was short-lived.

We waited for one more treatment before a follow-up PET scan.

Waiting for test results from a cancer scan is a special kind of awful. The results we received weren't great, but they were not devastating. The cancer had not grown or spread, but it also had not shrunk. We were back at square one. We were looking at three more rounds and then another scan. He had a blood transfusion because he was becoming anemic in hopes he would gain more energy. Unfortunately, this was not the case; energy did not return.

The tension building between each round of chemo and the uncertainty of waiting for tests to determine our future was racking. Benji's brother, Dan, sensed the need for us to escape. He sent us to Las Vegas for a short getaway. Although it was hard to travel, and we knew he wouldn't be able to walk much, we grasped the opportunity and headed to the desert.

We stayed at the New York-New York Hotel and Casino. My fragile memories only recall him sleeping the majority of the time while I sat alone in the heat of the shade near the pool. I agonized while normal life and joy swirled around me. This exaggerated my desperation to cling to a good and normal life. He had the energy to leave the room once, and we landed at a restaurant. We forced our conversation to feel like our old normal. We cherished our time together. We cherished our nights out and days away, and we wanted intensely to feel that again. But we didn't. Benji's mortality floated around us as we tried to talk about anything but cancer and how our time together may be limited.

We reminisced about our time in Boston just a few years earlier. We explored the historical sites, ate the seafood, and befriended the locals. Our short lives had been jam-packed with experiences. We remembered them fondly, but it felt as if we knew they would never happen again.

We talked about my mission trip to South Africa when the boys were very small. He transformed into Mr. Mom those two weeks and came face to face with all that I did for our family. We were separated, with little to no communication. He remembered feeling as though I had died—a small taste of my future.

When we returned home from Las Vegas, we jumped right back into the second round of chemotherapy, increasing to 100%.

Because of the increase in potency, we were hopeful for

change. Logically, making it stronger would be more effective, so we clung to this hope.

That and our hope in Jesus.

Benji's newfound faith was his foundation. He stood confidently on the grace and love of God and was able to shout to the world that God was good, no matter what. We both felt God so closely during that time. We read the Bible together, listened to worship music, and filled our home with the joy and peace of the Lord.

Unfortunately, the medication would cause panic attacks and anxiety, but despite that, we were surrounded and covered by Jesus. We both began seeing a counselor at church to help us walk through the uncertainty of his fragile life. Benji was ultimately terrified of leaving the boys and me alone. This was the torment that would wake him in the night. He slowly released those fears to the Lord and let peace take root in his heart. Our pastor reminded him that God loves the boys and me even more than he did, bringing him comfort. Once he could release that fear, he began to sleep more peacefully.

I was in a different place. I was not thinking of him dying; I was thinking of the joy we would experience if he lived. I had visions of us becoming missionaries and visions of Benji working with cancer patients to encourage them in their faith.

However, in reality, I had to face the possibility of him losing this battle. We had sorrowful conversations about what I would do if he didn't survive.

Our front porch was our haven. After the boys were in bed, we would often sit on the hard concrete steps looking out over our sweet, tree-lined street. One evening, he brought up the inevitable hard conversations that he was wise and brave enough to have.

"Heidi, I want you to get remarried if I go. I want you to move forward and raise the boys to love God. I want you to have a daughter." I sat one step below him and looked up, my face perched on my fist. I didn't have the words to respond. I needed to hear his words. I knew I would probably need them later, but I didn't want them to be real. With clenched eyes, I simply responded, "Okay." He needed me to acknowledge his relinquishment of me as his wife.

Amidst those rolling feelings of hope and loss, I felt peace. I was determined to live in the moment and to be grateful for his every breath. However, no matter how hard I tried, I couldn't control the outcome.

God was with us in those days. His presence was palpable.

We had some skeptical friends who claimed it was all in our heads. We were using our faith in God as a crutch to carry us through, but when you truly experience the love, peace, and presence of a living God, you simply can not deny it. It is something no human could conjure up. It is pure love. Pure peace.

During this time of treatment, Benji began to go to the office twice a week. We made the conscious choice to keep living as much as we could. If he felt well enough, it was a simple soccer game or a dinner out. We didn't want to waste one moment of our time together as a family.

As we continued with chemotherapy treatments, we continued to live in an abyss of the unknown. It was difficult to plan anything other than his treatments because we had no idea how he would be feeling on any particular day. But we tried. Some days, he would feel well enough to get out, but we also learned to live with disappointment and walked the earth one difficulty at a time.

I often fought feelings of resentment at the unfairness of it all. All the other husbands around me were healthy, working, and playing with their kids, while mine retreated to a dark bedroom, moaning for relief from his physical and mental agony. When he did make it to the office, it was often followed by a plea-filled call to pick him up early. I would sit in the parking garage, waiting for him to emerge from the high rise and climb slowly into the car, with a cloud of misery and shame covering his frail body.

He was fighting a lack of energy, a lack of life, and a lack of hope for a future not filled with sickness.

As the next PET scan approached, we decided we would seek a second opinion if the results weren't positive. We knew hope was diminishing with every round of chemo. This was an aggressive cancer with little to no chance of survival. Even if we were to defeat it, the chances of it returning were very high. But we kept fighting, kept hoping. We were not ready to succumb to the reality that his life was ending. We couldn't look each other in the eyes and imagine a world without each other. We were each other's world. How would I be able to breathe without him?

I had begun blogging our experince when Benji was diagnosed with cancer. Here is an excerpt from my blog May 2013:

We have decided to seek a second opinion if the scan results are not positive or only slightly positive. We are praying for God to lead us in the direction that he wants us to go and for Him to make it crystal clear. So, we wait . . . Monday . . . Tuesday . . . Wednesday . . . now, it's the day after tomorrow. Wait for the phone to ring. Wait and wait and wait. While I watch Benji sleep, have a drink of water, and sleep some more, I feel so helpless, so out of control, it is tearing my heart apart that I can't make it better for him. Somehow, find a treatment or cure that will give him life, not pain and agony.

As you can see, my mind is all over the map. I am confused, frustrated, and exhausted. Everything that I am dealing with is too much for a small person like me to carry. It is heavy. This is where my faith comes in. I struggle, but I am learning to lean on the promises of our great God to lead me through this shadow. I feel him close to me, and I have to discipline my mind to stop worrying and fretting and surrender everything in my mind to him. Everything with Benji to Him. I have begun doing this more and more in the last week, and I have noticed that my anxiety has lessened. I have been sleeping better, and I can control my thinking and turn it back to the almighty.

Here are some of the promises I repeat in my head minute by minute.

A Hard Journey to the Good

Be still and know that I am God.
Psalm 46:10

He makes me lie down in green pastures, he leads me beside quiet waters,
Psalm 23:2

But we have this treasure in jars of clay to show that this all-surpassing power is from God and not from us. We are hard-pressed on every side, but not crushed; perplexed but not in despair; persecuted, but not abandoned; struck down, but not destroyed.
2 Corinthians 4: 7-9

Do not be anxious about anything, but in every situation, by prayer and petition, with thanksgiving, present your requests to God. And the peace of God, which transcends all understanding, will guard your hearts and your minds in Christ Jesus.
Philippians 4: 6-7

Weeping may stay for the night, but rejoicing comes in the morning.
Psalm 30:5

No matter what I face in this life, God will never leave me or forsake me. Some say, "If tragedy strikes you, how can you say that God was there?" We live in a fallen world. God never promises we will never face trials and adversity, but he promises to be with us through them. I can attest to this with every fiber of my being. God has not abandoned us. God has not left us to fend for ourselves. God is here, in this house, in our hearts. God is giving us peace. We may not understand, but we TRUST God does. He knows the outcomes.

God is our refuge and strength, an ever-present help in trouble.
Psalm 46:1

Be strong and courageous. Do not be afraid or terrified because of them, for the LORD your God goes with you; he will never leave you nor forsake you.
Deuteronomy 31:6

I have a deep trust in our great God. No matter what happens, even the worst thing I can imagine, he will lead me through it and give me peace and rest. People often ask me how to do this. This is how I get through my days. I am not perfect, and my mind likes to wander back to worry and strife, but I always know where to go—to Jesus! This is how I wake up every morning and face this darkness. Jesus!

We had a friend from church, Mark, who worked at the cancer research center at the University of Utah. His wife, Melissa, was one of my dearest friends. Mark was one of those people who God wisps into your life the moment you need them. He was connected to renowned oncologists all over the country. As I stood on our back porch one crisp and sunny May afternoon, he told me we needed to be in Houston, Texas, at MD Anderson, a well-known hospital with next-level oncology. This thought was filled with uncertainties about the logistics and set me reeling with how we might make this work. How could we go to Houston? What about our children? Our house? Our dogs? Our life?

Thursday was the long-awaited PET scan to see where cancer stood. My nerves were on end as we waited impatiently for the results. We knew that we would get results either Friday or Monday. I wanted to know right away while Benji was afraid and wanted to enjoy the weekend (as much as he could) and find out on Monday. Well, we were both thrown off as we got a call from Benji's doctor Thursday afternoon amidst an emotional conversation about what the results may be.

He firmly told Benji that the tumors had grown and we needed to go in Friday morning to discuss other options. Our souls wailed with shocking disappointment. We paced the room, the tension palpable. We couldn't clutch the reality of the worst-case scenario. We hoped for a cure; we hoped for a miracle. We didn't understand how these last four months of intense and debilitating chemotherapy had not kicked that cancer into oblivion, with Benji's body clearly in dire straits. Chemotherapy was killing him. How could this cancer still be alive and growing? We interrogated God with our whys. However, we didn't have a choice except to simply continue walking into the fire, knowing the bona fide reality that God was with us in the furnace, this furnace of hardship.

We spent a sleepless night tossing and turning and woke up to a quiet and very sober morning. We drove thirty minutes to the doctor in silence. We both sat in the sullenness as we watched the living world pass us by as we were headed to yet another unknown terrain. We arrived and greeted Benji's beautiful sister, Erica, and waited.

The doctor's dire words sank into the room like a heavy anchor. He matter-of-factly stated that like he was giving us the weather report. The tumors had grown, and further treatment was needed. Feelings of resentment and anger were rippling through my mind as I witnessed this doctor ignore the fact that my husband could barely walk, breathe, live, or function as a normal thirty-something man.

More treatment and more poison was their only solution. I am not sure what I was expecting. I found myself resenting the entire atrocity that he had cancer at all.

We knew this was our cue to exit stage right and head to Texas. Our friend, Mark, worked around the clock coordinating the necessary logistics to pull this off behind the scenes in a realm of secrecy. We felt like we were part of an oncologist-seeking sting operation. We were given special permission to visit this doctor, and we smiled and nodded through each request.

The tiring process of phone calls, emails full of test results, and travel details left me reeling. I felt trapped as we were at the mercy of office procedures and scheduling at a hospital thousands of miles away.

The Sunday before we left, I encountered God in

miraculous ways through the people with whom God surrounded us. I went to the front for prayer after the service, and the woman praying prayed as if she knew me and every detail of our circumstances. She assured me we were doing the right thing and Houston was where Benji needed to be. My friend, Chris, called me that afternoon to encourage me to start praising God for His healing. I was filled with hope and passion for the adventure we were ready to embark on. The uncertainties were packing their bags, too, but we knew God would be with us every step of the way. I was lifted to the highest of expectations.

As the day went on, I became more confident of our place in Houston and began to just rest in Jesus, knowing He would continue working out the details. I could just sit back, relax, and watch it happen.

The next morning, I received the call I had been anticipating for days. I stood at our neighborhood playground, watching my innocent babies play tag around the jungle gym. Their little hearts were still oblivious to the dire place their family had landed.

They asked us to be at M.D. Anderson in Houston, Texas, June 6th, at 8:00 a.m.

Chapter 3
The One Where My Life Fell Apart

"If we hold tightly to anything given to us unwilling to allow it to be used as the Giver means it to be used we stunt the growth of the soul. What God gives us is not necessarily "ours" but only ours to offer back to him, ours to relinquish, ours to lose, ours to let go of, if we want to be our true selves. Many deaths must go into reaching our maturity in Christ, many letting goes."
Elizabeth Eliott [2]

A Hard Journey to the Good

A Hard Journey to the Good

In 2009, Benji earned an incredible opportunity to join a month-long tour of several European countries in search of places to store servers for his company. It was planned in a last-minute kind of fashion. I got online and purchased him a Eurorail pass, and he was on his way. He left me home with the two very small boys, off to an exciting new land that would fuel me with a deeper passion for exotic experiences. I remember feeling like this was the beginning of our lifetime of adventures. I longed to live in foreign places and travel the world. I longed to serve on mission trips and help others less fortunate than me in far-off places.

During the four weeks he was gone, I journaled every night, telling him of our simple life back in the real world. I shared what activities we had done, what I was feeling with him so far away, and how I longed to be with him. He celebrated his twenty-ninth birthday at a famous bar in Brussels, Belgium, called Delirium Cafe. He was thrilled to be there, and they served a beer that he enjoyed. He recounted a tale of giving the bartender his Utah Jazz hat and instructing the bartender to hang it on the wall. I often think of that bar and wonder if his hat is still there, declaring his once-present moment and celebrating his life.

He left a mark wherever he went. Once, on a Caribbean cruise, he traded one of his hats with one of the servers on the beach (you know, the men that serve the big umbrella drinks at an outrageous cost to unsuspecting tourists). He gave this hard-working man his Utah Jazz hat in exchange for a large straw hat. I remember being upset as it was not a fair trade, but I thought it was endearing because he knew he was leaving a little bit of himself there with that foreign man, who most likely doesn't get much attention from tourists.

After his European trip, he had the opportunity to visit China for several weeks, and months after that, he left us for a spell in India. He saw the world. I wasn't able to be with him because of our small children. But, looking back, I was willing to sit them out so he could have those precious experiences not knowing they would be his last and that we would never have those adventures together. Unknowingly, it gave him some of what he would need to find closure in his life here on Earth.

When he was close to death, he explained he felt he had lived a full life, even at the young age of thirty-three. He had married the love of his life, fathered two amazing sons, and seen the world. What else did he need? He would say, "I feel blessed to have had the life I had; I, of course, want more, but I am blessed."

Even though he was out galavanting across the globe, we had somehow managed to harness a sweet little life on Sherman Ave. We lived simply. We were not extravagant, and we certainly didn't pretend to be. We valued our time together and cherished what we had created.

Over the years leading up to his cancer diagnosis, he was living his best life yet. Traveling, working out regularly, eating what he should, and avoiding (at best) what he was supposed to.

One spring night, we attended a concert, something we did often. He was a massive fan of music. His interest in music developed his character as he continued to learn about new music from the underground circuit, and he often took me to small venues across the city to cheer on the humble entertainers. At one concert in particular, we found ourselves dancing near the stage, jumping, singing, and having fun. Afterward, as we walked to the car, he said breathlessly, "This is the best I ever remember feeling." I agreed with him as we hugged tightly, clinging to this rare piece of elation.

That memory solidified in my mind. When I think back over my time with him, he didn't feel good most of the time. I think I became so used to him feeling unwell; it just became part of who we were. I feel like the last few years were an anomaly. A sheer blessing from the Lord, a last hurrah of living on this planet. Perhaps this was so I could have something to hold on to. Something to share with the boys. The goodness of the Lord was flowing, we were thriving, and Benji was thriving. Until he wasn't.

We landed in muggy Houston, Texas, on June 5th. I slid Benji into his wheelchair and pushed him through the airport and into the hot southern sun. We checked into our hotel, just a few blocks from the hospital, and settled into our suite. We were blessed with a kitchen, so I could whip up healthy meals and snacks and limit restaurant outings.

We woke the next morning, drove the short distance to the hospital, and pulled into the valet at MD Anderson. We were immediately impressed with the level of order. We checked in and were sent to the oncology floor. The prospect of a miracle cure carried us to the place. We were sent away from Salt Lake on the wings of high hopes. The GoFundMe page with the photo of us at Weeping Rock was traveling through the internet, collecting the funds we needed for his treatment and our trip to Houston. We could not imagine this would not be our answer to the desperate, healing prayers.

We met Dr. Arthur, a small, thin man. Our story of suffering flooded out as we pleaded for help. We knew he was the so-called expert in this field.

We left feeling the meeting was anticlimactic and disheartening. The words that flowed from his young mouth were not as we had hoped. The doctor stated matter of factly, "We will begin testing and discuss the process of finding your treatment. This is a rare type of cancer, so we will do our best." His bland words didn't assure us Benji would be healed. He didn't raise our hopes of victory or calm fears of his demise. He was logical and unbiased.

We spent the afternoon being herded through the hospital from test to test, giving the doctors relevant information about his disease so they could curate a plan of treatment designed exactly for Benji's ailing body.

They told us to return in five days for a comprehensive plan.

We were now stuck in an unfamiliar city without our children. We were no longer on one of our whirlwind adventures; we were stationed at the hotel with little to no contact with the bustling metropolis just outside the foggy window.

The days slowly passed as we watched movies and read devotionals together. I spent time blogging my thoughts and sharing updates with the comforting community we left behind.

The tension was thick as we discussed how we would temporarily move so Benji could receive treatment. I spent hours on the iPad researching home rentals, schools, and all the things required to pull off such a stunt.

The search only left me in deep frustration as I threw the iPad across the room. "I need answers. I need to know what is going to happen." I silently screamed so as not to upset him. I was discouraged. Would we have to move or not? Would we need treatment in Houston or not? Would Benji live or not?

The realm of the unknown is not unlike stories we read in God's Word. The Israelites wandered in the desert for forty years, only being led by God's fire and cloud. They floundered in their faith but kept moving forward, blind and trusting the one true God.

Many times in scripture, God's people are left in darkness with only the light of Jesus to guide them. I felt like I was being led blindly through a sea of dark mud. The unknowns were slaying me, a slight glimmer of holy light to guide me.

After five long and agonizing days, we were finally sitting in the small, brightly lit oncology room, listening to the wisdom of Dr. Arthur. Benji's clammy hand held tightly to mine. His plan was more chemotherapy, and he informed us we would be able to get it administered locally near our home.

The good news was we didn't have to live in Houston for treatment, but I wasn't ready to hear it. I wanted something different. I wanted more climax and less letdown.

This was just more of the same. But this time, it was my wifely duty to find an oncologist who would be willing to administer the chemotherapy under the direction of the Houston doctor, and it would need to start pronto.

When we arrived home, I floundered in disappointment and frustration. How could we have left Utah with so much prospect to come home to a place without a doctor and only a slip of paper stating the type of chemotherapy Benji needs?

I lost all respect for chemotherapy. I knew it had healed

A Hard Journey to the Good

many people, but this was far from our experience. I only saw death and decay. I only saw suffering and false hope. How was more of this the healing answer?

I felt as though Benji's life was in my hands. It was up to me to make call after call to doctor after doctor, pleading with them to administer this chemotherapy to my husband promptly.

I was on the brink of a breakdown as I worried about his hydration, nutrition, weight, fever, blood pressure, heart rate, tumor, bowels etc, etc, etc. I worried he was giving up.

At long last, I secured an oncologist just minutes from our home. She was a tall lady with gray hair. She was gentle and sweet. Her office was dated, and the chemo was conducted in old donated recliner chairs. After the first meeting, she immediately sent him to the treatment room for his first dose.

After two days, he fell asleep for four days straight. His life was a purgatory—a dark room, static, surrounded by a spinning world. My heart ached for him, and I could see the agony on his face every single day.

Praising God did not come easy. It was the last inclination as I suffered, but I learned God is still good, even in the ugliest of life's offerings. Benji and I had been reading *A Thousand Gifts* by Ann Voskamp. She states in her book,

"It is in the dark that God is passing by . . . our lives shake not because God has abandoned but the exact opposite. God is passing by. God is in the tremors. Dark is the holiest ground, the glory passing by. In the blackest, God is closest, at work, forging His perfect and right will. Though it is black and we can't see and our world seems to be free-falling and we feel utterly alone, Christ is most present to us . . ."[3]

We don't choose our highways in life, but we can choose how we respond to them. Benji and I could have denied God's love for us and jumped into an even darker sea, but we chose to cling to Him as our life raft as the waves tossed us to and fro.

I realized I was beginning to grieve. I started to succumb

to the prospect he might not survive this, and I may be left alone, with two small children, with the untimely title of widow. I didn't like feeling that way. I didn't like how the word bounced around in my mind. It sounded foreign and awkward. I left these thoughts feeling guilty and ungrateful. I had to come up close and personal with the idea that my future hinged on his survival.

I wrestled with those thoughts and battled with the fear of the unknown. I would find myself imagining a life without him, a life alone, but would quickly retreat, as I didn't feel it acceptable to not have full faith in his healing. I felt guilty for thinking past his life into a new life, but for me, I needed to envision peace with him gone. I needed to know it was possible.

I strove to cling to God's promises of hope and life in scripture, but it was a walk of blind faith. God showed up in small ways as I gained respite in the chaos. I saw God's hand as he led us through those treacherous waters. Benji's faith kept me afloat as he encouraged me to trust Him no matter what.

I felt resentment in my heart as I knew he was going to heaven too soon, and I would be left in this earthly hell. I was the one who would ultimately suffer for his healing. I would be the one left to pick up the pieces of our beautiful, shattered life.

I had lost so much already. I was grieving who Benji was and what our life was before. He was no longer the man I married. However, I could sometimes see a small glimpse of him in his small idiosyncrasies and jokes tethered to pain. I held onto these moments with tenacity and gratefulness. He was diminishing before my eyes, and I was powerless to stop it. I had started a lifelong journey of missing him.

During the tumultuous weeks of the new treatment, we began to feel the absence of our cheer squad, the people who had surrounded us as we were lifted away to Texas. We came home to a lack of interaction, as if everyone assumed the trip was a complete success, and Benji would be okay.

I was the only person who saw the true nature of his well-being. I think God allowed us to feel a depletion in support so we could rely solely on each other and God. Benji whispered in my ear, "It's us against the world." It was us, alone, tethered, in the eye of the storm. Us and God.

A few weeks later, after several doses of the new chemo, I could hear the unsettling sounds of agony as I walked into the bathroom, only to find Benji throwing up something black and bleak. The dreaded sign of a blockage in his digestive tract. This was something we knew was a possibility. We knew his body could continue to get sicker and sicker. We both knew what this meant but clung to denial for the rest of the day, hoping and pleading with God to make it stop. We knew his next trip to the hospital could be the beginning of the end.

We finally succumbed to an ER trip, and as we waited in the sterile ER room for more test results, Benji struggled to talk in his gargling, sick voice. "Heidi, this is it. I am going to be leaving you." The words hung in the air like a fog. I couldn't grasp them. My consciousness floated without any stability, the shock wisping me into nothingness. I just laid my head on our clenched, entangled hands, no response necessary.

By the next afternoon, they had whisked him into emergency exploratory surgery after they confirmed that he did, in fact, have a blockage in his colon.

I found myself sitting alone in the waiting room of the hospital, stationed next to an old analog phone, waiting for it to ring with news from the nurse on how the surgery was proceeding.

After an hour or so, the phone rang. I reluctantly picked it up to hear the soft voice of the nurse gently say, "The doctor had to remove a large portion of his colon and replace it with a colostomy bag." My heart dropped. This was something that terrified Benji from the onset of his Crohn's disease. He longed to live a normal life, and he knew this device would steal what little dignity he still had left.

After the surgery, we spent that dark July night cornered in a sterile ICU room. I tried desperately to sleep on the hard, cushioned bench as the nurses came in throughout the night to deliver high doses of pain medication as his pain nestled at a 9 or

10 all night. His moans and rustles kept me half awake, half alive.

By the following day, his heart rate had returned to a healthy place, and we were moved to our own room. We were high on the fifth floor of LDS Hospital in a vintage crook of Salt Lake City. We had a clear view of old, rustic homes and large sycamore trees displaying a canopy of leaves across the old streets.

We lined the window with pictures and the flowers that were consistently being delivered. I was determined to spend as little time apart from him as possible, so I made a makeshift space for myself on a bench perched beneath the large window.

Since we were able to get scans sooner, we prepared for the news of how the chemotherapy was progressing. I called Dr. Arthur in Houston and updated him on the situation. He was very gracious and assured me that although we needed to take a break from treatment until he recovered, it was good that they had removed the diseased part of his colon. He informed me he would speak with our local oncologist when the new MRI results arrived, and she would inform me of the next steps.

I left the hospital to run home and check on the dogs when I saw the oncologist come up on my phone, and it rang with urgency.

I answered reluctantly, and her smooth voice echoed the words I had been dreading. "The tumors have still grown, and because of the dire state of Benji's condition, we do not recommend further treatment." The dreaded words crept from her mouth and through the phone like a ladybug crawling on your hand; you know it's there, but you can barely feel it.

She ended the conversation with the words you only hear in someone else's story, "There is nothing more we can do."

The words sat, nestled in my consciousness, without a movement. She whispered condolences and told me she would be organizing a social worker to assist us in setting up a hospice service in our home.

I was going through the motions and conversing about the process of my husband dying as if I were discussing my insurance policy. She said he may live weeks or months. But we needed to be preparing for my husband to leave us.

I left my home and drove to the hospital on autopilot. I dialed Benji's brother, Dan, and repeated the doctor's words. The other end of the line was full of silence and denial. Not only did I have to receive this tragic information and try to make sense of it, but I also had to do the horrid job of relaying it. I had to participate in the breaking of hearts and the tearing apart of lives.

I arrived at the hospital and rode the elevator to floor five. I intentionally caught this moment and held it with a tight fist. As the elevator rose, I recognized this was the beginning of my journey out of my beautiful marriage to Benji. This was my juncture, the one that would propel me into a new life. I didn't know what the end would look like. I knew I had to embrace this new reality I desperately tried to avoid. I walked into the room and sat next to my husband. I grabbed his cold, pasty hand and pulled myself close to him. I looked into his darkly circled eyes and repeated the slimy words.

"It's over. There isn't anything else we can do."

His response: "I know."

I think he always knew. He often mentioned the sinking feeling he carried that he would not live a typically long life. In those random comments throughout the years, it was as if he was preparing me, setting me up so that when the news did come, I would not be in utter shock. In some deep sense, I knew this would happen. I had envisioned myself as a widow long before cancer became part of our everyday vocabulary.

This was strangely and morbidly all part of the plan.

We spent two weeks navigating hospital life. We welcomed visitors, interviewed hospice companies, and planned his care to be waiting for him when he was released. The boys stayed with family, so I didn't need to leave him.

Benji turned thirty-three that week, his forever age. We rolled him down to the large, shaded patio outside of the hospital. Our family sat in the dry heat of the evening and soaked in his presence. We snuck him a small glass of whiskey and sang "Happy Birthday." We snapped a photo of his people surrounding his frail, sick body, limped over in his wheelchair, hospital gown, and socks with the rubber traction forever capturing his last days.

We were discharged on a hot August day. The sun melted through the car window as we made our way up the hill to our home. We were welcomed by family and nurses, all anticipating a crawl back to new normalcy before his body gave out. The unknowns lingered like a thick cloud.

We lived each day hanging by a thin thread, ready to break at any time.

Our home was constantly flooded with visitors and food deliveries. Our kitchen walls were lined with coolers of frozen casseroles and treats for the boys. Benji's love for God and the life-changing experiences he had while living his last days were the only things escaping his lips.

One afternoon, he sat on the couch, surrounded by co-workers, as he saturated them with the truths of God, His goodness, His care, and His unfailing love. The man I had dreamed of Benji becoming, the man I knew he could become, had arrived much later than I had hoped. This faith-filled man was always in him, but it took disease and death to bring it to light. It was now hello and goodbye to this new man.

As we shared the limited nights next to each other, I was battered with the reality that he could stop breathing at any moment in time. I would wake in the middle of the night, roll over quickly, and stare at his face—watching for his shallow breaths, reaching for his wrist to count his heartbeats, and looking for familiar signs of death. My Google searches resorted to researching ways to anticipate death and telltale signs that the time was approaching for Benji to breathe his last.

On the bright morning of September 4th, I wheeled him into Bonneville Elementary for the last time as we took Isaac to his first day of kindergarten and Jonah across the hall for his first day of first grade. We sat huddled near the classroom door as Jonah's teacher snapped a photo of us; little did we know, it would be the last photo of this clan. This last moment we captured the family we had created.

Each day brought on a new struggle or worry. His knees began to turn purple, and his memory started to fade. This once brilliant technological brain was now asking for help with simple tasks on his iPhone. He was lost in a confused realm of day and night, jolting awake at 2 a.m., telling me it was time to pick up the boys from school.

Benji rarely left his room, but when he did, he would join us in the front yard, where our family and friends had created a sanctuary of loss. He would slump into a chair on the porch, where he craved participation in any conversation, only to have him, moments later, express he was ready to go back inside.

Lawn chairs filled the grass, coolers of beer lined the sidewalk, and visitors pulled up to say their last goodbyes. I craved a sanctuary for Benji inside, a safe, quiet space for him to rest while the clamoring voices echoed through the open window.

We were essentially gathering to wait. Wait for him to pass. Wait for him to need care. Wait for him to no longer be with us.

One afternoon, we sensed the end was near, and I called Pastor Troy. He arrived shortly after, and when he entered our room, he found Benji sitting up, ready to converse. This left me confused and irrationally irritated. I was wrestling with thoughts of resentment towards Benji. I thought that if he was going to die, he should get it done already. No more of this waiting around, false alarm business. I needed to experience this, get past this, and start to rebuild my life.

I was in purgatory, and I found myself running out of my house, up the street, trying to excape the pain. Maybe if I ran fast enough, I would run straight out of my body, leaving the tattered skin behind. A lump of grief on the sidewalk that could be swept away and forgotten. I found myself huddled near the boys' favorite playground when my dear friend Tara found me, consoled me, and took me home.

I wanted to run further, faster. I wanted to escape this waiting hell and get out on the other side.

These feelings left me swimming in guilt.

I knew as I watched Benji suffer and prepare to die I myself was heading somewhere, too. I would tell people that it felt like I was waiting to walk into a fire. I knew it was going to burn. I knew I was going to suffer. I knew Benji was going to heaven, but I felt like I held a ticket to hell. But I was willing to walk into a fiery furnace so Benji could be free of his ailing body.

We read about the fiery furnace in Daniel 3. Three men, Shadrach, Meshach, and Abednego, refused to worship the golden statue that King Nebuchadnezzar had built, and their punishment was to be thrown into a fiery furnace. They were willing to risk their lives for the sake of God. The men stated, "If it be so, our God whom we serve is able to rescue us from the furnace of blazing fire, and He will rescue us from your hand, O king. But even if He does not, let it be known to you, O king, that we are not going to serve your gods or worship the golden image that you have set up!" (Daniel 3: 17-18, AMP).

The men had faith that God could rescue them but were also willing to trust Him, *even* if they were not saved. The three men were thrown into the fire. The King said, "Look! I see four men untied, walking around in the midst of the fire, and they are not hurt! And the appearance of the fourth is like a son of the gods!" (Daniel 3:25, AMP).

God allowed them to go into the fire, but He was with them in the fire. They walked out of the furnace unharmed.

During this time of letting go of Benji, I trusted God would be with me, *even if* Benji was not healed on earth. I knew God would walk with me into the flames of widowhood and help me to walk out. I knew the wounds inflicted by the fire of loss would burn, but I knew healing, redemption, and hope were possible if I put my trust in Jesus.

Shortly after this run-away escapade, his nurse Scott, after much begging, gave Benji a timeline.

Two weeks.

Benji wrote this final Facebook post:

A Hard Journey to the Good

This is an even harder update to write . . . grab some onions . . .

"Two weeks, then a week at a time."
I have noticed my strength dwindling and the desire to sleep 16 hours a day increasing. This, of course, is indicative of my body shutting down, resting, or generally just not doing well. I also have attained a nice shade of yellow on my face.

I talked to my hospice worker, and words that will resonate throughout my short life were spoken, "About two weeks."

9 months of riding the horrible cancer train is coming to a halt, and although my faith, my God, my loves, and my steadfast love of Christ remain intact, it's still very hard to grasp that this is the end. The hospice worker could be way off, and I hope he is, but that's the first date I have heard in this journey.

So, how do I feel about death? Quite simply, regardless of faith, dogma, upbringing, etc., death is part of life, a chapter that everyone will experience and one that few prepare for.

Being a person of faith, the passage feels easier—I know where I am going, and I know who I will spend eternity with. I hope that when the time comes, I approach death with strength and honor, just like I hope my life represents strength and honor.

I am very sad to miss out on my kids' upbringing, but regardless, I will be so proud of them in whatever endeavor they choose to embark on. We have raised them to be confident, free thinkers and to take life by the horns.

And to leave Heidi with the sole responsibility of a house, kids, and pugs. This is going to be hard, but the first promise God gave me after diagnosis was that he "has them" and that they would be taken care of. I have never let go of that promise; in fact, I see it manifest every day via huge outpourings of love, grace, money, and unconditional love. I seriously think I have the most loved family in the world. Thank you, God.

I have no shame in quoting Braveheart, "Every man dies, not every man truly lives."[4]

I absolutely feel like I have lived and accomplished my dreams. I have more, but that's ok. In my short life, I have traveled the world, fell and remained madly in love for 16 years, built a career where I was respected and did awesome stuff, and created two little miracles—Jonah and Isaac. I simply didn't allow room for regret, and I am happy for that.

In closing, life is absolutely beautiful if you stop and allow yourself to take it all in.

God IS good, even in a fallen, painful, cancer-ridden world. I implore you all to take creative measures in exploring this. God was absolutely real and shined so bright in the dark nights of pain and agony. He promised never to leave us and to be a comfort. He did not disappoint on this promise.

Always try to love by default; this way, you generally learn more about yourself and the source behind the conflict quicker and become a better person for it.

Not sure if I will update again. Please send any questions or thoughts my way and I will gladly answer them.

(Yell it with me!!!)

STRENGTH AND HONOR!

This time stamp on his life set us on the fast track to the end. Within the next week, Benji began to decline even more. He was sleeping twenty-plus hours a day and was unresponsive.

Benji's dad, Brent, and his wife, Kelly, stayed with us during that time. Brent took gentle care of his son as he struggled to grasp that he would survive his baby boy. Both of our families, our church family, and our friends carried us with their love and strength.

Even in Benji's almost trance-like state, he knew he needed to leave something for his boys. He wanted to write them letters. Benji needed help at this point with using the computer, but his sister, Erica, and his dad sat at the kitchen table, helping him type out the last words to his boys, the words they could cherish forever. Once those letters were complete, we saw a sudden decline. He knew that was the last thing he needed to do as a father before he could leave the earth.

Kelly sat me down on the couch one hot afternoon, looked me square in the face, and told me Benji was declining so quickly it was time to move him to a nursing facility; they could take better care of him. Benji had requested to die at home, but Kelly knew this was not the best idea at that point. We decided to nix Benji's request and set up his last hours in a place where I didn't have to live afterward.

I imagined an argument with him in my mind, and he agreed.

I stood in the kitchen as we discussed the logistics of moving him, and I was pummeled with the reality that when he walked out that door, he wouldn't be returning. I hunched over in defeat and wailed in sorrow at this disastrous ending to our life together, Brent, Kelly, and my mom standing on the sidelines, witnessing the destruction.

The next afternoon, as he slept peacefully, I went shopping to purchase new bedding and decor for my room. I told my mom I was desperate to change what I could, so I did not come home without him to a toxic room filled with medical supplies and dirty sheets. I was already craving new, craving fresh, and craving change. She bravely took me shopping as my husband was breathing in his last days.

This was my first widow experience as I chose a flower-lined comforter and yellow-striped curtains. I chose a pink wooden bird for my nightstand and a blush pink throw. I didn't realize it at the time, but I was living my life as a widow while he still lay at home. I was already disconnected and severing my life from his. The pink decor and floral accents screamed my rushing for independence from this pain.

For the rest of the afternoon, I lay by his side. I knew he was expected at the nursing facility at four o'clock, so I fought to wrangle my thoughts into appreciating and realizing the truth of this precious time. I played our lives in my head, like a movie, as I listened to our favorite music. I soaked in my heart, mind, and memories and did my best to honor our life together in those quickly passing minutes.

As the time approached, I told him it was time to leave. He was confused and weak. I held the pugs up to his yellow, sunken face so they could give him one last kiss. Yoda and Vader were our first babies. We got them one year apart, and having puppies gave us the experience we needed to start our family. The dogs were a source of comfort for him in his darkest days. He cherished the puggies, and I knew I would not only have to parent grieving children but also nurture grieving pets. I gave them what little closure I could.

I walked him out our back door and down the few steps to the car. I opened the car door and slid him in. All the while, he asked where we were going. I tried to explain, but it seemed absurd. The truth was nonsensical. *Oh, don't worry, honey. Just taking you down the street to die.* It was such a normal task. Get in the car and go somewhere. But it usually isn't forever. I participated in this menial task with life-altering implications as if I were going to the grocery store.

As I drove down 13th South to the facility, I prayed over him. I expressed my love for him and how he was going to a better place. Our last moments alone were anticlimactic as his soul was already halfway to eternity. We checked in, and as I laid him in bed, he kept repeating, "This is ridiculous, this is ridiculous." He knew he wasn't at home.

Benji was a nerd. A big nerd. One thing he had on his

radar in his last days was the Comicon Convention that would take place on September 5th. It would have been his greatest joy to take his boys to introduce them to all his favorite superheroes. The hospice facility caught wind of his desire to take Jonah and Isaac. As the day neared and the realization lay heavy on all of us that he wouldn't be able to attend, they arranged for the boys to go. Dan and Jesse were invited too, and that afternoon, they were all picked up in a giant red fire truck.

After I dropped off Benji at the hospice facility, I sped home to catch the action. Life and death were all taking place at the same time. I lifted my excited boys into the big, red truck and buckled them in. They all drove away with the loud siren blaring loudly, aching hearts striving for fun and normalcy, while Benji lay dying a few blocks away.

I immediately headed back to Benji.

He was carefully monitored that evening, and at midnight, after a flutter-filled sleep, I woke up to find him missing. I followed my instincts down the hall and found him wandering. He was still tethered to this Earth but ready to meet his maker, searching for his new home.

The next day, my own physical suffering was making itself known. I had lost weight and refused to eat. My mom tried to spoon-feed me scrambled eggs, but I could only down a few bites. "Heidi, you need to eat. Your body needs nourishment," My mom calmly encouraged as she watched as half of her daughter was dying.

I laid on the bed next to Benji, cradled in my mom's lap, and wept the cry I would later name the widow cry. A depth of sorrow poured out of my body in heavy convulsions and loud, aching wails. My mom stroked my hair as I was being stretched and yanked and pulled from my husband. He was going somewhere I couldn't go.

As I came to after my near-death tantrum, I mustered up the only strength I could to get the boys from school. We did not have a big yard, so we often borrowed a big, grassy spot on the fourplex property next to us. This space housed a large pine tree that we chopped down years earlier, and the leftover stump served as the home base for many family softball games. We played many games of tag and red rover in this space, and in the winter months, this was the best place for impromptu snowball fights and home to many Edmund family snowmen. The fruit trees lining the property were perfect for little-boy climbing and hide and seek.

When we arrived home to a daddy-less house that afternoon, I sat the boys down on the soft late summer grass, our favorite play place, and explained to them that daddy wasn't coming home. I gently asked if they wanted to say goodbye. I didn't want to assume their little eyes wanted to see Daddy in his final days. Jonah gave a resounding, "Yes, I want to see Daddy." Isaac responded much differently, refusing to visit Daddy. This serves to be a place of regret and sorrow for my Isaac. In his teenage years, we have had devastating conversations about his wishes that I would have taken him despite his resistance. I have to give this regret to the Lord. I did only what my mama's heart told me to at the moment, which was to respect his wishes and not take him to the hospice facility to say goodbye. Isaac has lived his life with barely a memory of his daddy and no sense of closure. I pray that one miraculous day, my son will find peace with his five-year-old self and find the closure that he needs.

That evening, I left Isaac with my mom and drove Jonah to the hospice facility. Brent and I wheeled Daddy out to the courtyard, and Jonah gently held his hand. As we sat out in the warmth of the summer evening, Jonah caressed Benji's arm and repeated, "Daddy, Daddy." His little heart was saying goodbye to his hero, his person. Benji was unresponsive as he sat upright, staring straight ahead. Although Benji was unable to grab Jonah in his arms, bear hugging him the hardest goodbye imaginable, Jonah still cherishes that small moment and clings to the meager closure that he was gifted.

I took Jonah home and left him and Isaac with their uncle Kurt, heading back to the hospice house with every unknown raining down on me. Benji was passing into another realm. I had followed him, cared for him, and journeyed with him until he would need to turn around and gently explain I could go no further. My soul reached a level of death, the farthest place a human soul can go without dying. I met him there. Sat with him there. Felt with him there. Lingered with him in the space between life and death.

That evening, I lay, cradled next to him. Trying to capture the essence of his existence, his presence, his all. He was cold and unemotional. I wasn't going to leave this spot until he did.

The rest of the evening was spent in prayer and worship. We read the Psalms and welcomed his best friends. They sat next to his responseless body and said whatever their hearts could muster. The pastor prayed. We awaited the inevitable torture of loss.

At midnight, as we all discussed who was going to stay with him or where each of us would sleep, he began to gasp for breath. His oxygen level was dropping. His body was participating in the act of letting go. He was packing his things for his next journey.

We watched him breathe sluggishly. My mom read a poem about heaven, and his response was a surprising fist in the air, agreeing in the excitement that that was his next stop. We turned on his favorite song, *He Loves Us* by David Crowder Band, as I cuddled his struggling body in this agonizing state. I kept telling him that it was okay to leave. He was free to escape his failing body. God would take care of us. We would be okay.

Finally, at one point, I had the urge to sit up and look at his face. A flash of white light filled my perception of the room, and he took his last breath. Brent's hand rested on his young son's heart as he said gently, "He is gone."

At that moment, I took back my words. I shrieked through tears, "It's not okay, it's not okay. Come back! I can't live without you. Come back."

The wails erupted, and his sister said loudly, "He is seeing the face of GOD."

Worship music was playing. With cries vibrating off the stone-cold walls, we all held this moment as if we could harness his presence and bring him back to us.

As I realized life was gone from his body, I could not get out of bed fast enough. I took one step. I captured the reality of the moment and said under my breath, "My first step without Benji. My first step into a life without him. Here I go."

I walked to the other part of the room, where someone gave me a side hug. As I walked towards the door, I lost consciousness, fell sideways, hitting my shoulder on the door, and smacked the ground, full body colliding with the hard, carpeted, concrete floor.

The months of grief, the months of worry, the months of caretaking, and the months of loss all let go. My body let go. I allowed myself to sink into a death of sorts. The death of my life with him. The death of my other half. I quietly lay there as I could hear the concerned whispers of the people surrounding me.

I knew that opening my eyes and sitting up would be the final acknowledgment of Benji's life. He left. He was gone.

And now I have to get up and keep going.

Chapter 4
The One Where I Was a Widow

*"I'm convinced that there is nothing that can happen
to me in this life that is not precisely designed
by a sovereign Lord to give me the opportunity
to learn to know Him."*
Elisabeth Elliott

A Hard Journey to the Good

God does incredible work behind the scenes of our lives. As we get older and have more life experience, we can look back and see where His hand guided circumstances to make His plans come about.

I had always been a dancer and longed to be a cheerleader. Before I decided to change high schools, cheerleading tryouts were coming up, and I knew I had a slight chance of making the team. My parents and I agreed that I would move to a small private school on the other side of town if I did not make the team. I wanted to pull my head out of the clouds and make better choices for my future. This cheerleading tryout would be God's way of telling me which direction to go.

I practiced my heart out, and when it finally came time to stand in front of the crowd of parents and perform the routine, I froze. Not just forgetting a few moves. I froze. Solid.

The coach stopped the music, motioning me to start again. I froze. Again.

Needless to say, it was ultra humiliating. I am sure my Dad was in the audience cringing at watching his daughter fail so wretchedly. I was devastated and embarrassed, and I came to terms with the idea that my time at Cottonwood High School was ending, but little did I know about the new life that would emerge. God allowing my muscles and mind to freeze at that moment was an act of His mercy and taking control of my life, something I came to terms with many years later. God knew the trajectory He wanted my life to go, and He knew it would take a heartbreaking humiliation to get me there.

By the following fall, I was accepted on the small cheerleading team at Salt Lake Christian Academy and well on my way to a new life and a new school, surrounded by the people who would encourage me in my walk with the Lord. This is where I met Benji.

These are the events that began my journey of life with Benji, which ultimately led me to the hospital floor in utter despair seventeen years later, having lost half of my soul.

The world was now Benji-less. It still is, and I still find myself in shock that he has disappeared.

I gathered enough strength to sit up and rest against the cold wall. With anguish pulling me down into despair, I rounded up the last bit of courage in my soul. Swimming through the broken fragments of my life just to get off the floor took every ounce of energy I had left in my frail, dying body. But amidst the torture, a small seed of hope was striving to take root. I was relieved. The wait was over. The moment I had been dreading for months was now in the past. I did it. I said goodbye to my best friend. I took a deep breath and vowed in my heart to keep living.

My first cognitive thought was to call our best friends, Scott and Kami, in Minnesota. They knew the call was coming, and I am sure the phone ringing at five am shocked them awake, knowing the words to be said from the other end of the line.

I could hear the muted and tired "Hello?" on the other end of the line.

"He's gone."

I could hear silence and muffled cries at the expected yet shocking news they just received. Our foursome was now a trifecta.

His mama, Leonie, spent time adjusting his body, closing his mouth, and nurturing him for the last time. We each said our goodbyes.

After everyone had said their goodbyes, I asked everyone to leave the room so I could be alone with him or what was left of the man I knew. I grabbed his cold hand for the last time, looked at his sunken and sleeping face, and uttered my last words to him, "We did it. We ran the race. Now, you are home. We will be okay."

As the sun rose that cool, fall morning, we eventually emptied the hospital room and said our goodbyes to the human form of the man we loved.

The foggiest memories of going to bed in my newly decorated bedroom that early morning with my mom by my side only flitter in my mind. I was unable to hold a thought or create a real memory.

That evening, we gathered at my parents' house. Being together held us upright. If we were alone, we would succumb to the devastation and may not choose to move forward.

"You are being held up by the love of these people," my mom said that night as I rested my head on her shoulder.

We all gathered on the front porch and watched the newly released Coldplay video of "Atlas." Coldplay was the soundtrack of our life together. We knew every song. Every album. We listened to Coldplay on repeat on road trips and warm summer nights in our backyard. For them to release a new song the day he died, a song about loss and new life, was not a coincidence. The Lord knows that music is an avenue in which I sincerely feel things. He knew I would need something tangible and audible to hold on to.

In an unfortunate turn of events, Jonah's birthday fell the day after his daddy took his last breath. This was something that Benji held onto and tried to control in his final days. He didn't want to die on Jonah's birthday, but he didn't want to miss it. We had held an impromptu birthday party two weeks earlier to calm Benji's nerves about the precious boy who needed celebrating without the cloud of loss dampening the joy.

We celebrated Jonah early and spent an afternoon at Chuck E. Cheese with close friends and family. We mustered joy and celebration for the little man, and Benji sat on the sidelines, frail-boned in his wheelchair. I headed all the bustling about with presents, cake, and candles. But he was there. It was the last birthday Benji would ever celebrate for his firstborn. He partook in the festivities the best he could, and Jonah can now hold on to that. He cherished seven little boy birthdays with his daddy.

Although we were all living out of scarcity, we again celebrated Jonah on his actual birthday, the day after Benji died, at his Uncle Dan's house. My bleak memory sees Jonah standing over his cake with our closest people belting "Happy Birthday," so loudly exaggerated as if we could penetrate heaven.

We dared not say we felt relieved that Benji was now in heaven, especially amidst his baby's party, but we were. We all felt a deep breath of respite after the harrowing days we had just escaped. We were all glad to have the worry of Benji's wellbeing behind us and knew he was safe, healthy, and whole. He was now in the arms of Jesus. His absence was penetrating, but on this day, we chose celebration.

The following day, Benji's family and I sat in Stark's funeral home's floral decorated waiting room, surrounded by pamphlets of caskets and flowers. Soft music played as we all floated out of our consciousness.

We are simple people. Benji was a straightforward person. We didn't need extravagance, just something uncomplicated that would represent him. We followed the funeral director up a small flight of stairs to a loft filled with many caskets. Benji loved all things space, so as soon as we eyed the silver casket, likened to a spaceship, we pointed, giggled, and agreed.

"That's it," I said. Everyone agreed.

We had quickly chosen the space to encapsulate his body for all time. This was it? His whole life coming down to where he would lay forever? We struggled to tear our human understanding of him from his body to it now being an empty vessel. Why did we need to do anything with it at all? The unsettling traditions of humans baffled me, and I found only nonsense in all of it. I could hear Benji saying, "Good pick on the rocketship, but why waste your money?" I agreed, but this is just what we humans do. We conjure up activities that can help us curate any sort of closure.

The twisted practice of celebrating a life already lived weighed massively on my shoulders. Thankfully, the funeral home took that load and worked hard to present his life graciously. We chose tropical flowers for the casket and simple bar food for the celebration of life. Nachos, brats, hamburgers, beer. We were working hard to create a space all about him. It would smell and taste like him, but one thing would be missing. Him.

I was instructed to go home and fill boxes with all his

things. He was a man of many interests, so the boxes filled as I tossed in everything he was in our home. This included Star Wars and Lord of the Rings trinkets, stacks of books, technology, beer making, snowboarding, world travel, and faith. I spent that evening shuffling through thousands of pictures and putting them on a small drive so that the funeral home could create a slideshow to present throughout the celebration. I did it all. I did it without thinking. God created shocking numbness for the bereaved in all of His brilliance. The human body would not be able to handle the reality of the loss in those first few days. We would crush under the weight. He layered us all with a sense of peace that carried us through these days of planning and remembering.

The Celebration of Life was on September 10th. That afternoon, my sisters came to my home so we could all get ready together. We wore our superhero/nerd shirts per Benji's request. We walked to the shopping center near my home to the hair salon blowout bar so we could all get our hair done. It felt oddly like a group of girls getting ready for a dance or a wedding, not a funeral. The girl asked me what the occasion was, and I was forced to blow her away with the fact that I was getting dolled up to celebrate my dead husband. Over the years, these awkward conversations with strangers became normal and less uncomfortable . . . for me. But watching strangers wiggle in their skin as they try to find the words to converse with unrelatable me has never settled well.

I pulled up to the funeral home. Benji hadn't taken a breath for seventy-two hours. I stood outside and called my kids to me as they climbed out of my Dad's car. Jonah scurried across the parking lot, and I noticed he wasn't wearing shoes.

"Jonah, where are your shoes, buddy?"

"I forgot them, Mom," he replied matter of factly.

I felt a wisp of frustration, but instantly offered grace. I would have to quickly get used to dealing with minds that did not function correctly. We were no longer working at total capacity, and scattered-brained was our new normal. I felt a surge of pity for my young boy. He was a vision of sorrow and trauma. A few weeks earlier, when Benji started to disappear in tangible ways, Jonah took on the coping mechanism of twisting the front of his hair, and after many weeks of pulling, a small bald spot appeared near his hairline, visible evidence of a boy who lost his daddy. My vision of my hairless, shoeless boy is nestled in my memory as the epitome of motherly grief, our pity on display for friends and family.

I took my boys' hands, and we walked into the room with the casket, barefoot and all. Benji requested the casket be closed, which I gratefully agreed to. With all the other essential yet excruciating traditions we were participating in, I did not want to look at my dead husband's body for an entire evening.

The room was gloriously filled with his possessions. The astonishing funeral workers had taken the contents of the boxes and displayed them perfectly. I still cannot grasp the genius behind sorting through strangers' belongings and making beautiful sense of them. They printed the photos and framed them according to their kind. One section was family, framed photos of our small unit, and everyone who loved us.

One section was snowboarding. His coat, boots, and pants hung next to photos of our days on the slopes. We had taken lessons in our thirtieth year, learning something new together as grown adults. We spent many days on our backsides laughing at our pain and discomfort.

We continued to meander through the room. I followed the wall slowly, step by slow step. One section was our wedding. One section was his love for music. One section was all of our travels—all the framed photos that had been displayed in our basement. The others were filled with his hobbies and interests. His collected memorabilia was set along with photos and certificates. He came alive in that room. Everyone who walked in that evening was bombarded by his presence, taken aback in breathlessness. His nearness was something we were still not used to living without. His music played the essence of him; he leaped out of the perfectly curated sections.

Just down the hall, slideshows played in the large back

room, and people stood around bistro tables as the waitresses held trays of his favorite food and beer. My shoeless Jonah and silly Isaac ran waist-high through the crowds with their friends, their laughter only a surface of their existence, the shocking blow of their daddy gone lurking underneath.

The director positioned me in front of the door and instructed me to stand there for the beginning of the event to welcome the guests and allow them the space to come face-to-face with the one person they would try to avoid—the widow.

The title of the widow was trying to weasel its way into my being. I had yet the time to grapple with the word after only three days in, but I knew it was plastered on my face. Remember the last episode of *Seinfeld*, where they are on trial, and each character from the show's nine seasons appears to testify? Sans the courtroom, this was what was playing in my mind.

When in one's life are we in a room with everyone we have ever encountered? What kind of person gets to mingle with everyone who helped shape your life? A widow at her husband's funeral, that's who. This ironically privileged moment was mine. I welcomed people from all walks of life. I hugged people from our high school and the several churches we had attended. I embraced co-workers of Benji's who had been in our lives for minor seasons. I allowed childhood friends, neighbors, and far-off relatives to cry on my shoulder as they offered their sincere condolences. I stood solitary, dying inside, in a space surrounded by life with a smile on my face. I was the lone widow in a room of Benji-grieving people. I took in the smiles, the tears, and the weight of hundreds of bereaved. I caught the tears of others as they flowed down my cheek, hitting my black shirt donning Batman, Benji's favorite superhero.

I whispered to the director to retrieve my lip gloss from my purse. I was on. I was the star of this bizarre production. I stood erect while my husband lay enclosed in a flower-laden casket just a few steps away.

At that moment, I felt like an empowered superhero. I wore it well. I stood tall. The inside of me was not yet aware of the journey of widowhood that was mine and mine alone, A trip I had barely taken one step into.

Classic rock blasted as the night wore on, getting louder as the beer continued to pour. My brother Nick and other musically talented friends tore into a jam session with drums and guitar. We swayed our sadness away as we took in the photos as they slid by on the big screens. We laughed. We cried. I begged people not to forget about me.

I stood embracing Benji's siblings. I felt the weight of sadness from my siblings. The unknown of how they would handle their now-bereaved older sister encircled their minds. My parents mingled with lifelong friends as they took in hugs and condolences, living the nightmare of losing a son-in-law and having to catch their daughter from falling into the nothingness of widowhood.

Benji's parents gathered condolences from strangers and friends alike. Their ears took in soft words of admiration for the spectacular man their baby boy had become.

The following day was September 11th. I stood in the bathroom and stared in the mirror at a widow, breathing, but only because she didn't have a choice. I was wrestling with the fact that I was getting myself ready for my husband's funeral. It had been planned out. The music, the photos, and the speakers were perfectly curated to represent this man who had touched many lives.

The funeral was located at Capital Church. Our safe space. The place where we grew in our love for the Lord. The place where I made friends after becoming a mom. The place that supported us with counseling all those long, cancer-ridden days. This place would cradle our sorrow on this cloudy September day.

Now, little did I know, there is a reverent way to walk into a funeral. There is an order. It is expected that the tormented, barely breathing, barely walking widow must present herself first, displaying her grieving, dying self to everyone she has ever known.

A Hard Journey to the Good

The boys walked in with me. It felt strangely like a wedding procession. The similarities were creepy and horrific—one procession filled with hope and one with dread. I clenched the boy's hands and could feel hundreds of eyes blaring into my back as I walked down the aisle through the hushed crowd. Every person was relieved they were not me, the wives clutching their husband's hands tighter.

I wore a black, sleeveless dress with tall black heels. That dress still hangs in my closet, the black fabric collecting almost a decade of dust. My hair was shoulder-length with wispy highlights and soft curls. My brother told me I looked like the widowed Jackie Kennedy that day.

I imagined the news headlines of a celebrity widow sighting. "The tortured widow walked behind her husband's casket, gliding in strength and grace. Death and turmoil writhing inside her body, hidden behind her soft smile and glistening eyes." I only wished I had Jackie's black face covering that day, shielding the world from the misery struggling to leak out as I desperately tried to keep it at bay. My boys wore slacks and button-downs with Old Navy loafers. Their hearts and minds were unable to fathom the gravity of this process. They just followed the instructions and sat where they were told, unaware this was the finality of their life with a daddy.

We sat down—a front-row seat to the grand finale of Benji's life. Benji's casket was nestled under the stage, a stage that housed many sermons that helped shape our lives and gave us strength in our most challenging times. That day, the church was not filled with Sunday morning churchgoers sipping their Starbucks or Tazo tea. That day was filled with grieving hearts and crushed souls.

Pastor Troy took the stage and, in his carefully crafted words, told of a man who he knew well in times of joy and turmoil. He witnessed Benji's leap into faith and knew that Benji would only want his final hurrah to be centered around the good God who carried him through a whole life, into sickness, and on into eternity. "The family wants everyone to know they are not angry. They trust a big God who sees what they cannot," Troy said in his stoic and comforting way. This platform was Benji's way of sharing His love for God and the incredible ways He had shown up for him and his family. This was Benji's way of making his most significant impact on the world, even after death.

We had invited several of Benji's closest friends and family to speak: Benji's dad, Brent, his best friend, Jesse, and Josh, the company owner into whom Benji poured his life's work. These men spoke of a man with integrity, a man of love, and a man with a purpose. The words infiltrated the room and the hearts and souls of all who attended.

The service ended with a slideshow of his sickness journey to "Let It Be" by The Beatles. Shock and awe took over as people gasped at the unsightly appearance of a cancer-ridden man. But they also witnessed the ways God showed up in the tragedy. They saw Benji surrounded by family and friends, and even in his darkest hours of pain, he could still conjure up a smile or a snuggle with his babies. His pale and yellow skin peered through the large screen, screaming death, but Benji's legacy called for life. Life with God is more significant than cancer and succumbing to disease. This was what he wanted everyone to walk away with.

When the service was over, we ambled out of the church, greeted by the hearse. The casket slid into the back as a small group of us headed to the cemetery for a private graveside service with his closest people. I rode with my sister, and in a cliche and movie-like fashion, it was raining. We trailed behind the hearse for a few miles as it pulled into the Murray Cemetery, where my grandparents and uncle are buried. I spent many days in this place mourning the loss of those who had gone before me. I have pictures of me as a small child at my uncle's funeral, and I remember Benji standing there with me as we buried my grandfather. This was a familiar place that felt safe to leave him.

The large tent was set up over the grave, and the hole had been dug. Umbrellas surrounded the space as small whispers were heard amidst sniffles and cries. We all watched as friends and brothers pulled the silver rocketship out of the hearse and labored up the small hill, casket pulling down on their arms. The strong men carry a strong man. They laid the box above the hole, resting on the mechanism that would soon lower my husband into the ground. Troy spoke more gracious words about my husband.

I had never envisioned us being there as they lowered him, but we were. It was as if we all wanted to be there until the very last moment we could. In an impromptu motion, everyone grabbed a single tropical flower from the top of the casket and dropped it into the hole where my husband lay. A pile of broken flowers piled up, a visual of the lives that he had touched. We lingered. We cried. We hugged. We grieved.

The casket now lay in its final place at the bottom of the six-foot hole. Benji's dad grabbed the shovel, gathered some dirt, and poured out the first layer to cover his son.

It was then time to walk away and leave him. I knew he had left me long ago, but this was the final separation of who I knew him to be. This was his final resting place, and it was time for life to begin without him. The significant acts of closure had come to an end. Nothing was left to do but walk away and begin a new life.

His closest friends and family gathered at his brother Dan's house afterward. It is one thing to get together as friends to celebrate, but this was different from any other party we had thrown or attended. This was grieving people, hurting people living in the denied reality of loss, drinking their sorrows away. And that is what we did. I had no hesitation about downing the shots and pretending everything was okay and everyone else was in the exact same boat.

We were Benji's people, but he was not there. He was missing, and we were tripping over ourselves all night trying to calculate and articulate how to live without this man on all levels. The widow, the parents, the siblings, the in-laws, and the best friends, all about to embark on our own journey of grief while simultaneously trying to handle everyone else's sorrow gracefully.

Parents grieve differently than spouses, spouses are different than siblings, and siblings are different than friends. We would battle out our own loss while grieving alongside each other, being careful not to compare and contrast our suffering. This was going to be challenging at best and life-sucking hard at worst. We didn't know what we were in for, but we had no choice.

The night ended with me being carried to bed, only to wake up the following day with my first hangover of widowhood. I called my Dad early in the morning and asked him to rescue me. He took me back to their house, where I had stayed the entire funeral week. They had graciously let me and the boys live in their space during these tumultuous days of saying goodbye.

Dan, his wife Jaime, and I had agreed the night before that we needed to get away to ease the pain. We spontaneously booked another trip to Disneyland. Why not hop on a plane and get outta dodge? Travel proved to be my coping mechanism in widowhood.

I had always been a nervous flier. Nights before a trip, I would lose sleep, conjuring up every terrifying scenario and holding on for dear life as the plane ascended into thin air. This never stopped me from traveling, but fear overtook me until I could order cranberry vodka to calm my nerves.

Well, one benefit of experiencing your worst nightmare is that nothing else can scare you.

I was no longer afraid as the plane took off the day after the funeral. It was the opposite of being scared; I wished the plane would crash. I was hoping to die. With each movement of the aircraft, I hoped it would start falling. Then and only then would I be put out of misery.

I shifted in my seat as I was slammed in the face of what had just happened. It all came crashing into my heart and soul as I sat confined to the soft airplane chair. I could not escape the painful nightmare that entangled me. I wrestled and fidgeted, unable to stand being in my own skin. The flight landed in Southern California, and I glided through the motions of travel without any wherewithal of how I got there, drifting in and out of conscious reality, going from one activity to the next, following Dan and Jamie, who were drifting through the chaos of loss in different ways. They had a job to do. They had to take care of the widow. And they did. They cared for my fragile being even as they forced themselves to stand on two feet. Somehow, by God's grace, we were not face down in the airport bar.

We stood in line at the Grand Californian Hotel. There were people in front of me and people behind me. I stood there, anxious to get to the hotel room and pop another Ativan. This acute anti-anxiety medication took the edge off of the perpetual rattling in my whole body. I shifted from foot to foot, unfamiliar with my new self, aching to crawl out of the tight space of grief.

Grief wasn't recognizable yet. I wasn't used to these out-of-body experiences; all I craved was escape. I would learn years later that this hurting girl, standing in line at the hotel, would be the girl I would want to comfort when I knew for certain she would be okay.

Disneyland was a blur. I wish I could recall the small moments of joy we were all able to grasp. I am only left with a few pictures and Facebook posts. The smiles on my boys' faces were sincerely broad but underlying with a sorrow so deep they could not yet reach, a sorrow so deep it would take years to pull out.

As if Benji's death and Jonah's birthday a day apart weren't enough to pack into this lousy month, I also had the unbelievable task of living through our wedding anniversary, September 15th, our second day in Disneyland.

I floated through the day, wondering which way was up, a walking mummy. By dinner time, we were sitting at a picnic table in Frontier Land, waiting for our BBQ spread to be served. There was a cute couple singing country songs, and they asked the audience if they were there celebrating something special. They mentioned birthdays, promotions, and the dreaded word. Anniversary. Really? I thought I was being inconspicuous, holding back my tears. The patrons of Disneyland were none the wiser that I had just been widowed, but then, they had to come right out and ask if it was anyone's anniversary. I could sense the tension between Dan and Jaime as they eyed each other, not sure how I would respond. I tipped my ball cap down over my eyes and let the tears fall, the pain to seep, the reality to be faced. God knew I needed to truly acknowledge this day and not allow it to flitter by. It was those little moments of acknowledgment that led to healing. Even if they are excruciating, they carry us to new levels, each and every one of them.

This was the first anniversary or milestone that I had to face, only eight days into my grief journey, and I got the most painful one out of the way first. In a sense, I was relieved it was over.

After three days in California, we arrived home to a husbandless and daddyless house. A house needing repairs. A house needing a computer update and a furnace filter replacement. The unchecked hubby's to-do list now had my name at the top. The endless responsibilities of a household fell on my weary shoulders.

The first Monday home was the first "regular" day. The boys went back to school. I tore myself out of bed and began the familiar routine of motherly life, but the shackles around my ankles weighed heavy on my frail body. I had yet to gain my health back. I needed more stamina, strength, and motivation. My lungs moved up and down involuntarily, the only part of me keeping me alive. My hands moved through tasks from memory, not from any sense of purpose. I was transported into a foreign life, forced to navigate unfamiliar territory.

Benji and I often had the ritual of going out for breakfast on Saturday mornings. We would slowly awake and chat in bed about where we wanted to go. Frequently landing on our favorite local place, Eggs in the City. The people, the food, that vine-covered patio always welcomed our small family. The first Saturday back to real life hit hard. I sat up in bed, and the tears and sobs flew out without warning. My boys heard the sobs and came in to snuggle me. I held my boys with loud wails as I grieved that small tradition and knew we would never get it back, not with Benji anyway. It was one of a million tiny little losses I would have to learn to wade through.

One afternoon after our trip, my mom was at my house helping me navigate my new, terrible life. She walked into my room and found me pulling all of Benji's clothes out of the closet. She asked in shock, "What are you doing?". I quickly responded as I pulled shirts off of hangers and pants out of drawers, "I can't stand to look at his clothes anymore". This was my room now, and he was no longer welcome. Every widow handles loss differently, and because I had spent the last nine months saying goodbye, I was ready to say goodbye to his things. I was mad that he left, and this was my revenge. I placed his things in large plastic bins and carefully stacked them in my room. I wasn't ready for them to be out of the room, just out of sight. A little while later, I saw that my mom had moved the bins to the basement. I was angry she hadn't asked me if that was ok. I am sure it didn't make sense to her. It didn't make sense to me. Nothing made sense anymore. Life was a mess.

After several weeks, I found the boys and I pulling up to the Sharing Place: A Place for Grieving Children. Someone I knew had recommended we join the group to gain support in our new loss. We got out of the car and slowly walked up the giant steps leading to a big porch wrapping around a white brick house.

We grabbed the ancient, brass door knob, and the door slowly creaked open. We walked inside to the old, musty smell of the aging house, finding our way to the living room. The small area had mismatched couches and chairs wrapped around the walls. We were welcomed by loving and gracious new friends who asked us to sit. The boys sat on my lap, snuggled up and nervous, not understanding why we were in this place with these strange people.

The adults sat in the living room and spent the two hours sharing about their losses and encouraging one another while the children were taken downstairs for activities to help them cope with their loss.

I found myself stiff-necked, striving to keep tears at bay as the reality of where I was and why I was there sank deeper into my body. I was there because my husband died. I was there because I was a widow. I was introduced to other widows and men who had lost their wives. Each story was different, and as each person shared, I felt safer and safer.

I was so thankful that the boys were loved on and invited into a safe space for children who had lost a parent. They felt normal there. They felt seen and heard in their pain. The boys did art projects and jumped around the volcano room, which was covered top to bottom in padding so they could express their aggression with yelling, banging, and pillow fights. This was their favorite part of our time at the Sharing Place.

As we left the facility that first night and walked out into the dark, cold, late fall air, the dread of life was again upon me. Driving home in the dark, getting my sleepy boys inside to do the bedtime routine alone, again, was lonely and depressing. I was so sunken in grief I had to grasp with all my might to even slightly understand God was with me in those bleak, chilling moments.

Just around the one-month mark of losing Benji, my sister-in-law Jaime learned of a new podcast called *Loveumentary*. The two people who started it traveled around the country interviewing couples and asking them to share their love stories. She contacted them, and they agreed to interview me for their podcast. They were intrigued by my story of love and loss.

They came to my house just as I was having new furniture delivered. We sat at my tall, black dining table, which was new and right out of the box. There weren't any scratches or paint chips. There wasn't food stuck between the crevices, and it hadn't yet been christened with years of meals and laughter.

They placed a microphone in front of me and began to ask questions. I was in a delicate state, and as soon as the man asked me one question about Benji, I dove head first into an hour-long spiel about our life together, including all the gruesome details of his death and my new widow life. It felt good to tell the whole story. It felt good to be seen and heard. It felt good to allow all that yuckiness to leak out in hopes it may encourage someone out in the world.

Years later, I would scour the internet for the podcast, and when I found it, I listened to the fragile, frail voice. I felt a deep ache for that young girl—the girl who had yet to heal, the girl who had a million miles of life to live without any direction or capability of seeing past the loss.

With the podcast and my blog, I felt a release when I shared my story. I gained readers on my blog, and with every post, I received an array of comments, encouragement, and prayers that gave me the fortitude to keep going.

I was thankful for the community around me. My dear friend Vanessa and her family lived behind us and supported us daily. She was there when Benji was sick and when he was gone. We would walk our kids to school, dissecting my life circumstances and striving to figure out how I was to maneuver in this new life. She listened and stayed by my side through all of my widow-brained moments.

I had my friend Josh. He is a lifelong friend. We joke that we were friends in the womb. Our parents were friends before we were born and are still friends today. I cherish our late morning breakfast dates, where he would intently listen as I poured out the mysteries of loss, and he would have deep, meaningful questions, causing me to think hard about the complexities of my new journey.

Benji's group of friends was solid and brotherly. He was intentional about rallying them all to take care of his widowed wife and children after he left. His last words to them included the protection of his family and his expectation they would be there for us.

Unfortunately, he left a hefty obligation on their shoulders, one that seemed impossible for them to live up to. They felt a responsibility to check in on me and take the boys to the vintage arcade. Benji envisioned his friends taking his place in some odd way, not understanding how much of an ask that really was. Several of them helped me remodel my bathroom. That gave them a sense of peace, knowing they were helping me in a tangible way. In years to come, I would rely on them less and less, leaving some of them with feelings of guilt that they weren't there for me anymore.

Sara, my therapist, was a solid rock for me. I met with her in her office several times a week. One day in particular I remember looking out the window at the beautiful fall colors. The reds, oranges, and yellows billowed out of the trees, something I usually took delight in. But I was no longer capable of enjoying beauty. I told her I didn't have it in me to delight in anything. I felt guilty for even a sense of joy, even a simple fall breeze or a brightly glowing tree. She listened sweetly and nodded thoughtfully as I sobbed, realizing that fall was now tainted with loss, something I knew I would have to process every year, forever.

Grieving is so complex, and it isn't as linear as Benji thought it might be. He didn't account for how everyone would grieve differently, how seeing me and the boys was a knife in their already broken hearts. Jonah and Isaac were a brutal reminder of what was lost. To some, it brought comfort; to others, it brought pain. My relationship with some of his friends dissipated. The glue was gone. This is no fault of anyone except death. There are no hard feelings; it is just the nature of deep loss and traumatic life change. I am forever grateful for the men who stepped in those early days and comforted a grieving widow in the best way they knew how.

When a widow is born, she faces losing her husband, and many friendships morph and change. I clung to many friendships that held me up, loved me, supported me, and even stood by me when I began to build a new life. They were there no matter how uncomfortable it was for them to see me change. They still are, and I am forever grateful.

Unfortunately, some friendships disintegrated because our connection was lost or people felt uncomfortable in a friendship without Benji. Over the years, I learned to dole out loads of grace for those lost friendships.

Chapter 5
The One When the Shock Wore Off

"Time doesn't heal. It's what you do with the time. Healing is possible when we choose to take responsibility, when we choose to take risks, and finally, when we choose to release the wound, to let go of the past or the grief."
Edith Eger[6]

A Hard Journey to the Good

A Hard Journey to the Good

Although my boys are only nineteen months apart, the place of development in which they lost their daddy was evident in their abilities to cope with the loss. Jonah was seven, and Isaac was five, clueless and unaware of the nature of permanent loss. Jonah could grasp a bit more and had his grip on me. He was petrified of being left at school. His tiny first-grade teacher tried to hold him down while I attempted to leave each morning. After a few days and weeks of this pattern, I could see the exhaustion in the teacher and recognized the disruption for the class. One cold morning, I trudged into the school office and whispered, "Help." I needed help. The principal replied softly, "Honey, you don't need to do this alone. We are here to help you. Come to the office every morning, and I will help you get Jonah to class." I was relieved to be seen and heard.

I was ill-equipped to handle this component of motherhood. I was drowning in guilt and anguish. I knew Jonah needed a sense of normalcy, but it felt brutal and unloving to leave him at school crying for me. After several weeks, Jonah began to relent and was able to saunter into Mrs. Okabe's first-grade class with more grit and healing under his belt.

Isaac, on the other hand, was still young enough to enjoy Kindergarten. Mrs. Barrett walked my boys through this trauma, as Jonah was in her class the year before when Benji was sick. It was a safe place for Isaac, and I was thankful for that. At the elementary school, the boys could earn Bobcat Bucks, pretend money they could spend at the school store. One afternoon, as I helped Jonah get his things out of his locker for the day, he pulled out a small plastic measuring tape and inscribed on the front it read, "My Dad Rules." He handed it to me gently and said, "This is for my new dad." My throat closed, and my eyes watered as I held back tears. I could see a small glimmer of hope in my precious little boy. He knew there was life on the other side of loss. There was hope for another man to fill the daddy's shoes even as he was deep in grief. His innocent anticipation propelled me forward.

Life at home was peculiar and upside down. Bedtimes

weren't as strict, screen time restrictions were lost, and my ability to say "no" left along with my title as a wife. However, we began to gain a bit of traction with a new way of life, albeit crazy and upside down, with the sole purpose of surviving. The boys would fall asleep in my bed, one on each side nestled into the crook of my arms. The blood slowly drained from my hands as they drifted into a dreamland where, hopefully, Daddy was still alive—a place of reprieve for their weary little souls.

Before the chaos settled in the evening, Isaac insisted on playing dead and needed me to revive him. I learned this was his way of coping and coming to terms with the permanency of death. I played along and pretended to do chest compressions and mouth-to-mouth. He would come alive, and I would rejoice. He was trying to understand why his dad never came back to life. Maybe by returning to life himself, a small part of Daddy would come back, too.

Before the boys drifted to sleep, we prayed small, simple prayers. We prayed God would bring us joy again and one day he would bring a new dad and husband. In their small hearts, they knew a new dad was something they wanted. It didn't take away from their daddy in heaven, but they simply had hope in their hearts.

As the boys drifted off to sleep, I would lay there, eyes plastered to the ceiling, knowing that I had only a dark evening of loneliness awaiting me on the other side of the wall. I would slip out from underneath their heavy, sleeping bodies, walk into the dead, quiet living room, and sit. I would stare and think as my mind calculated the enormity of my new life as a widowed mother.

We had a silver clock positioned near the kitchen. I would watch the secondhand move slowly around the clock. Each tick-tock indicated one more second on top of thousands that he was still gone. Each second represented a life farther away from the one I knew with him and screamed of the permanency of his absence. Each tick solidified my widowhood.

Facebook scrolling was my solace as I tried to climb back into memories long gone. I would play "Oceans" by Hillsong United on the TV and lay on my side staring at the lyrics.

Faintly, I would whisper my thoughts to Benji under my breath: "You are missing our life. Where are you?" I was desperately pouring my soul into God, the only thing on this earth that I knew was solid. Everything around me wobbled and swayed. God was steady, real, and my anchor. He was in the business of keeping His promises, and I was eagerly sitting in the front row, waiting to see how He would turn this turmoil into good.

Romans 8:28 reads, "And we know that in all things God works for the good of those who love him, who have been called according to his purpose." I knew these words. I'd heard them a million times, but I was now anxious to see God actually come through for me in this way. In my brittle state, I could not see past the darkness of night let alone imagine a new, fulfilling, purposeful life awaiting me. It was abstract and nonsensical to me, but I chose to believe.

There is a verse in Philippians 4:6-7 that reads, "Do not be anxious about anything, but in every situation, by prayer and petition, with thanksgiving, present your requests to God. And the peace of God, which transcends all understanding, will guard your hearts and your minds in Christ Jesus."

I had always heard this verse and loved the words, but I wasn't entirely sure it was possible in the severe storms of life. However, one night, as I lay in bed, wearing Benji's shirt that I had taken from a stack next to my bed, I felt it. A sheer peace. A peace that I didn't understand and one that I certainly didn't think was possible. It was otherworldly. But it happened. I felt God's hand on my life and the life of my boys, and in that small moment, I knew we would be ok. We had hurdles and mountains to climb, but we would be ok. And perhaps one day, find joy in a new life. I was thankful for this moment and still carry it with me today.

Not only was I being remade, but I also poured newness into my house. This is how I coped. I needed everything to be mine. I craved a space that didn't remind me of him. I needed a jumpstart to a life as a woman living without a husband. I don't feel regret for the instant change of scenery. This is how I processed it. I sold our furniture, and although it carried precious memories, it reeked of death. I filled the home with new couches and a new dining table and hired my brother-in-law, Kurt, to repaint the kitchen and living room. I purchased new lamps, unique wall hangings, and printed black-and-white pictures of our whole family to display.

At some point, I knew we needed to go back to church. It was like returning to the scene of the crime, but I knew keeping that part of our life alive for the boys was essential. Walking into church, as expected, I was bombarded with tight hugs and "How are yous?" Others who didn't have that kind of courage gave a slight nod to acknowledge the grotesque un-relatability that oozed out of my skin. I was a widow. It wrapped around me like a tight sweater buttoned up to the top, almost choking me out. But even in that awkwardness, I held close to my church community. They were there when Benji was sick and died and were still there for me now.

These early days of widowhood are hidden in a blurry mess in my mind. I know they existed, but I blocked out a lot. I try to remember how I got up in the morning, got the kids to school, and even slightly functioned like a normal human. My Facebook messenger was full of messages I had yet to read. I had stacks of cards in the kitchen. I had a fridge full of frozen meals. Benji's brother, Dan, and his wife, Jaime, hired a cleaning lady to come once a week. This was one of the most helpful things. Coming home to a fresh, clean house after running errands was more than I could have asked for.

A friend came to my door one day, and the ring jolted me out of bed. I appreciated her concern for me, but I was not in any space to talk. I felt bad being blunt, but I just did not have the capacity. One afternoon, I found a box full of yellow and sunshine-themed items on my front porch, and fresh flowers lined the bookshelf. It lasted a while, but then it slowed down; the flowers died, and the messages stopped. Everyone else had continued their normal life, but I couldn't. My normal died.

I learned when someone is suffering from loss, the most important time to reach out to help them is long after the funeral and first weeks. They are most likely flooded with concern, but when it wears off, that is the most difficult time. Loneliness sets in, and they feel forgotten. I have remembered this over the years and remember to reach out to fellow widows on all the hard milestones days, and I always want them to know they are not forgotten.

My parents were my rock. They released their daughter to her new husband thirteen years earlier, and now, they had the responsibility of my care and safety planted back into their hands. My dad was eager to help me around the house and repair things that had been left for too long. We had a carport that needed to be enclosed, and he spent one Saturday afternoon with my brother-in-law, Waid, building me an enclosure and a shed. My mom, sister, Chelsea, and I spent that day at a festival in the mountains. On our way home, we got a call that my dad had injured himself, and they were headed to the hospital. We were given vague details and told to head back to my house.

I left my dad in charge of a new couch delivery, and I knew the new leather couch was sitting on my front lawn, ready to be stolen. These types of hiccups didn't frazzle me when I was married to Benji, but my already staggering vulnerability made me uneasy and anxious in this challenging, scary situation.

When we arrived home, the couch was safe. We asked a neighbor to help us carry it inside and waited for a call from Waid. The neighbor had commented on our house being the "party" house, as he had noticed weeks earlier how many people had been fleeting in and out and hanging out in the front yard. I am sure it was odd to all the renters who surrounded us . . . if they only knew.

As we waited for my dad to arrive back from the hospital, we began to worry because it was taking longer than expected. A few hours later, my dad sauntered into the house with his hand bandaged and proceeded to tell us he had cut off half of his thumb as he sawed wood for the enclosure. Waid walked in with my dad's shirt on, which was much too small on him, and he had to give up his shirt to wrap Dad's hand. Waid told us he had to pick up the thumb, put it on ice, and take him to the hospital. They were not able to salvage the thumb, but my dad was okay, and Waid was traumatized. We weren't sure what that experience meant, but at this point in our grief journey, nothing surprised us. Life was a crazy twist of circumstances, and we now laugh about this crazy day. Life was happening, and things were taking place, but Benji was not a part of them. The list of things to tell him grew longer every single day.

Four weeks passed in a flash. I found myself face down on the cold kitchen tile, sobbing in agony. I felt the urge to scream as loud as I could. The torture was begging to escape. I screamed loud enough for heaven and the neighbors to hear. I repeatedly listened to "Atlas" by Coldplay as if I could summon Benji's presence. I was only left with memories. Nothing new about him was tangible, and I was getting further from him with each wail.

A few hours later, I boarded a plane headed for sunny California to visit Benji's younger sister, Alisha. We both found ourselves single again, as she had just gone through a separation from her husband. Once, the four of us had been close, and now here we were, husbandless and single.

We lay belly down on the beach, staring into the vast ocean, wondering what had happened to our lives. I read excerpts from a book I carried with me by Carol Cornish called *The Undistracted Widow*. This book was my comfort in my early days. I copied widow prayers from the book and took them with me for months. There was one in particular that I recited about loneliness. I was reassured in this prayer that I was not alone in my widow's journey. I had a loving and faithful God who knew the depths of my pain, was willing to work on healing my pain, and was ready to meet me in the darkest shadows of my new life. I felt alone, I looked alone, but I was not alone. God promised never to leave or forsake us, and I held onto this truth with gritted teeth and clenched fists. I knew it to be true even as the storm of loss raged around my tattered soul.

Joshua 1:9 states, "Have I not commanded you? Be strong and courageous. Do not be afraid; do not be discouraged,

for the Lord your God will be with you wherever you go."
God instilled in Joshua otherworldly courage to overcome the battle he was facing. God charged him with taking God's people to the promised land. Joshua felt unequipped and unprepared, with only three days to prepare. However, God reminded Joshua that this was His perfect plan. God allows hardships and enables challenging situations, but He never leaves us alone to fight the battle in our own strength.

God was calling me to live a life without Benji. He charged me with tearing down the walls of my old life, kicking out the insecurities and fears that weighed me down, and learning to trust God would rebuild my life. My promised land was coming. My job was to continue trusting God, even in my loneliest, darkest, and most painful moments. I clung to Him, and I was encouraged to keep pushing through.

God was instilling in me a bravery I had never known. He was pushing me past my limits but also right there beside me, championing me and giving me hope to see past my anxious thoughts about where He was leading me.

During my stay in California, Alisha and I rented bodyboards. We pushed through the heavy waves out into the cold water, and I wrestled with the metaphor of how my life felt now widowed. Each step was hard and heavy. I turned around and waited for a wave big enough to ride. One wave I rode smoothly to shore; the next pummeled and threw me spiraling, upside down and backward, leaving me breathless and confused. These are the waves of grief, unpredictable, unreliable, and ever-changing.

One warm evening, we went to a nice restaurant nestled in the harbor of Newport Beach. We dressed up. Single girls now. However, singleness didn't fit right. It felt awkward and uncomfortable. I hid behind the familiar comfort of the platinum ring on my left hand. I hid my new widow identity, and inside, I was bursting.

We sat at a bar, sipping a cocktail, and waited for a table. The familiar jeering and itching I felt on the plane that first week after the loss and the out-of-my-skin moment at the hotel tortured me. The memories of Benji and me dressed up and enjoying adulthood were tormenting. I sat unsettled as Alisha tried to handle my raw emotions. She, too, was navigating the loss of her older brother. She had feelings and torment of her own. Together, we were a perfect storm of misery.

I traveled home and back to the tortured reality of life alone. I dreamed of Benji. I dreamed of talking with him in our kitchen as we shared hugs and tears. My subconscious was still clinging to his earthly presence. It would take years for my dream state to catch up to the reality that he did leave.

During these tumultuous weeks, my brother, Nick, moved in. We had a spare bedroom in the basement, and having another adult in the home was comforting—someone to pick up the slack and help me navigate the logistics of caring for the boys. My sister, Chelsea, would come over during the dark fall evenings and sit with me on the couch, watching Friends reruns. She helped me escape the loneliness the best she could. Friends was a source of solace for me. I could climb into the TV even for a few moments and numb out my own reality. I could perhaps form a small giggle at the jokes I'd heard a million times, but it was a temporary reprieve. As much as I wanted to escape my gruesome reality, it was impossible.

My friend Vanessa shared with me that during those first weeks, it was harder to get me to laugh. My mom told me recently I was trying to cover up my new widowed face with too much makeup, something that was so unlike me. She just let it be, hoping the new me wouldn't try so hard.

Remember that scene in *Men in Black* when the alien takes residence in a man's skin to try and look like a human? His wife says to him, "Edgar, your skins hangin' off your bones."[7] That was me. A grief alien was trying to morph into my skin, trying to look like a normal person. A person with a normal life. A person that wasn't dying inside. I was barely recognizable as the new me was wiggling and squirming, trying to find its way out.

I tried to numb the pain with retail therapy, a very

common but temporary respite for widows. Swiping my card at Nordstrom Rack as my cart filled with goods I could not have afforded before somehow gave me a feeling of normalcy, but it was short-lived. A pain medication that wore off by the time I reached the car.

Losing a person in their bodily form is one thing, but they still remain in so many other states. He still lived in the unopened boxes of his stuff from the celebration of life. His belongings were still in cardboard in the depths of the dark basement until I dared to open them. As I gained the fortitude, I opened the boxes one evening and found him popping out to say hello. His things, his smells, the only things left of his life on earth. I closed it in shock as if I had opened the doors of heaven.

On October 24th, I journaled I was driving on a clear, rainless day, and out popped a rainbow—a little love note from beyond. I walked into the grocery store to hear "Rocket Man" playing, one of our favorite songs. I imagined texting him and letting him know these things. I think I did text him after his death. It was instinctual.

On October 29th, I posted, "I have never been addicted to a drug, but I think what I am experiencing is similar to those going through withdrawals. I am desperate for a hit. I need him. I need to hear his voice and feel his touch. I am anxious, nervous, sweating, and wanting to climb the walls. I need a fix, man! I need a fix. I wish I could relapse. Oh, what I wouldn't give." I blogged and posted all my real and raw feelings. I would feel all the emotions welling inside me until I opened the valve of words and let it spill out, relieving me from the pressure of loss—a force that would have caused me to burst.

Around week seven, my frozen existence started to thaw. My fingers began to tingle, and I began to feel things in the most painful way possible. I could no longer hide behind the shock; I was now forced to face my new reality head-on. My therapist, Sara, told me that not only did I need to start facing the reality of the loss, but I would also begin dealing with the trauma of watching Benji suffer and die. I was forced to dig through layers and layers of complex emotions and realities, and trauma would be another word added to my daily vocabulary.

The boys and I started the ritual of therapy just before Benji passed. After he was gone, I was determined to give my boys every opportunity to process and heal. I would see Sara separately and take the boys once a week. The psychology of grieving children fascinated me. It wasn't "sit on the couch and talk about your feelings"—it was, "Let's play on the floor and see what comes up."

During one of our first visits with Sara, Jonah crawled underneath a chair in the waiting room and refused to come out. Graciously, Sara climbed right under there with him. She soothed the hair-twisting boy with soft words and assured him this was a safe space. That session seemed ineffective then, but that is where he was in his healing journey. He could not reach out; he needed someone to reach in.

Isaac would play his familiar game of dead and alive again on the carpeted floor of Sara's office. She observed their play and assured me they were doing precisely what was expected of grieving children. I am not sure if the fact my kids were suffering 'normally' comforted me, but I took the information nonetheless.

I spent a weekend with my boys in Minneapolis in early November, visiting our best friends. I began to sense a pattern in my drinking habits. I would drink without reserve, feeling temporary relief, but feel the weight of grief compounded tenfold the next day. Anxiety can be exaggerated with alcohol, and since I was already carrying a heavy strain in my daily life, alcohol felt suitable for a little bit until it wore off. I saw the pattern, but I didn't care. I was in such a tormented state the idea of changing habits or taking away coping mechanisms was not something I could pursue.

After I returned from Minneapolis, I was invited to a comedy show with Benji's siblings and some friends. I anticipated the night as I knew some of their friends were single men. This oddly excited me, even though I was still fresh off of a loss. I had not been touched, kissed, or hugged romantically for over a year since

Benji and I's intimacy stagnated when he began to get really sick. I was feeling things I never anticipated so early in the widow game.

John was my sister-in-law Jaime's family friend. He had recently lost his father and was a source of comfort and understanding for this grieving family. He was handsome, tall, and sweet. It had been over sixteen years since I deemed myself available to be flirted with, and when he touched the back of my neck as we walked out of the restaurant, I was flooded with unfamiliar endorphins.

After the bars closed, I found myself at his house. We talked through the late night, and in silence, he reached over and kissed me. I had not been touched and loved for so long, and I melted into it. However, even in my most vulnerable state, I felt resistance and asked him to take me home. I didn't allow it to go any farther as I could see the emotional and spiritual implications a mile away. He dropped me off at my parent's house, where my boys were sleeping, in the wee hours of the morning. I was left reeling. Reeling from guilt. Reeling from new feelings. Reeling from a newfound freedom to be loved by another man. Combined with a heavy hangover, I tossed and turned that early morning as I wrestled with the new skin I was forced to wear.

It was now oddly okay for me to seek attention from another man. I knew the limits, but I also relished the freedom. Unfortunately, along with that came mounds of shame and guilt. I had only been widowed for two months. What was I thinking? What would Benji think? I was determined to keep the incident a secret. However, I released the information during another alcohol-induced night, and the news hit the fan, shattering the family and compounding the atrocity I had committed. Judgment entered my story that day. Judgment was my new battle. Widows have a brutal war to fight as they strive to survive their new normals. And judgment took a front seat for me.

But no other person in my realm knew what I was feeling, experiencing, or living every day. Other married people had their spouse next to them every night. They could be cuddled, touched, or kissed at any moment, but I could not. The idea I had kissed another man was a deadly sin in everyone's eyes.

No one talks about the physical and sexual loss that comes with the death of a spouse. The desire would be so strong in moments that I would feel like climbing out of my skin. Trapped in desire with no way out.

The amount of loss a widow must endure is ever-lengthy. According to Lisa Appelo, a fellow widow blogger, a widow faces the loss of their partner, inside jokes, strengths, family, plans, shared past, expected future, shared dreams, traditions, normal, youth, confidant, loss of home, co-parent, intimacy, physical security, dreams, friends, financial security, identity, anniversaries, couple friends, routine, decision help, best friend, and income.

All of these losses happen in one moment when a widow's husband takes his last breath. Of course, I didn't realize the sheer depth of life change that would enter my life at that moment. These have all been discovered over time. He died, along with a million other things. Benji's wife died and was slowly being brought back to life as someone new. I was in the business of becoming unmarried

I was unsure what this incident meant for my friendship with John as I certainly was not ready for a new relationship, and I knew I would see him again. I decided to take the step to call him. We talked and left it open for something to possibly pursue in the future, but for now, we were content in our friendship. This experience left me with a peace knowing my widowhood would not be a deterrent in the future to find a life with someone new.

In late November, I finally felt I needed to do the necessary tasks to finalize Benji's resting place. I called his brother, Dan, and asked if he wanted to go with me to design and pick out Benji's gravestone. I was thankful he wanted to help me, as it was not something I felt equipped to handle on my own. We drove downtown and sat in a small, musty office as they explained to us the different varieties of gravestones and what our options were. Together, we designed something simple with engravings of a cross and a large image of Saturn covering most of the stone.

Benji was fascinated by all things space and science,

and one of his final words to all of us was that after he was gone, "you will see me sitting on the rings on saturn." He knew after his time on Earth, he would be heading for a bigger and more vast existence.

The two of us spent many dark nights, with his body failing, hashing over what heaven is like and how he longed to ask God all of his big questions. After his passing, and well into the years following, we would often see NASA's most recent pictures of Saturn, each one more and more detailed, displaying for us the vastness of God, demonstrating for us His miraculous creation. Benji was a more intricate part of all of it. I could see him floating through the rings in perfect peace and wholeness.

Saturn is a significant reminder of the person he was. Placing the image on his gravestone was the perfect way to commemorate him. It wasn't until January that it would be placed in the ground, freezing his place on the earth.

As a widow, I was starting to gain independence I had never had before. When I got married, I moved straight from my parents' house to Benji's house. I had never lived alone and had never been in the place financially that I had as a widow. Thankfully, Benji set us up to be taken care of, so I never lost my house and never had to go back to work. However, with that financial freedom, I had a lack of accountability. I didn't have Benji asking me about my spending, and I didn't need to ask anyone if it was ok if I went shopping.

Right before Jonah was born, we purchased a sage green Subaru Outback. It was brand new and fully loaded. I loved that car. It was a perfect family car for our small family, and we spent countless hours and many road trips nestled in the cream-colored leather seats. When I found myself as an only parent, I started to think about how, at some point, the boys would want to bring friends with us on outings. I sensed the need to trade in our beloved Subaru for a bigger car. This was also a way of letting go of my life with Benji. I needed something new.

A few weeks before Christmas, my brother Nick and I headed to the car dealerships on the other side of town. I had my eye on a 2013 Honda Pilot. After the salesman walked me around the shiny, new car, explaining all the amazing safety features, I was sold. I told them I would give it a night to pray about it. The idea of spending a large portion of the money I was left with took time to swallow. I prayed about it, and the next morning, I was still unsure if it was wise to spend the money, but God gave me peace. I drove down to the dealership that morning, traded in our sage green station wagon, and drove away in a brand new dark gray Honda Pilot. I let the tears fall as I drove back up the hill, leaving another part of Benji behind. This was just another step into my life without him. Shedding our life together, piece by painful piece. We now had a nice, big vehicle for new adventures, whatever the future held.

In the final days of Benji's life, my dear friend Tara and her husband Greg gifted the boys and me round-trip tickets to Maui for Christmas. We would travel with Benji's brother Dan and his wife Jaime, their children, Benji's baby sister, Erica, and our friend John. I skirted around the plan-making as Benji lingered in his last days. I was unsure how to tell him we were making plans without him as he still breathed. However, he was aware. He knew he was leaving, and we would need to have an escape for the holidays. I can hardly imagine his thought process as his family was planning a future without him as he sat in the next room.

I love Christmas—the twinkling lights, the music, the decorations, the traditions, and the feelings. Benji and I created a precious life full of sweet memories. And in the few short years we celebrated together with our boys, Christmas morning had been magical in all the ways it could be.

After he was gone, Christmas time was a special kind of torture. I refused to listen to music, decorate, or participate in holiday merry-making. I knew we would be in Hawaii on Christmas day, so I had nothing to prepare. I neglected my neighbor's gifts of treats and steered clear of busy malls. I was able to sneak past December partially untouched by holiday gladness.

We arrived in Maui a few days before Christmas, and as

we landed, I was flooded with memories from our honeymoon just over thirteen years earlier. Pushing past grief forces us to relive memories and face the hard things. As much as Maui was a reprieve, it was also heavily laden with blissful honeymoon remembrance.

We were only twenty when we married and had never been on a vacation without our parents. Benji booked the trip with a travel agent, and we had everything set. However, learning to travel well and spend wisely was a life lesson we would never forget. We had received cash at our wedding, which was allocated as our spending money for the trip. We had no clue how fast a quick grand would be gone, and as I handed my debit card over to a cashier in a gift shop on one of the last days of the trip, we soon realized how fast it goes. We were broke. We had spent every last cent and then some. We were in the hole, in a far-off land with no way to purchase anything else. We were too prideful to call home to ask for money, so we skimmed by on the small amount of cash we had left. We made it to our last day, and as we sat in the airport waiting for our red-eye flight, we sifted through the last of our change at a small table. Benji was kind enough to let me spend the last couple of dollars on an ice cream cone, proving, again, we had a lot to learn. But we learned together. We grew together. We matured together. Now I was left navigating a Benji-less life, all the life lessons ingrained into who I had become.

The boys and I arrived at our hotel in Kaanapali late, and I laid the boys down to sleep. I had an ocean-view room and sat on the balcony, taking in the salty ocean air. At that moment, I sadly realized even though I had not intentionally packed up my grief, it boarded the plane with me, bringing along anxiety and loneliness as its carry-on. I could not escape my nightmare. Grief was my new, annoying best friend.

The two weeks in Maui blurred by. They were filled with beach days and whale watching and topped off with my first panic attack after I tried my first puff of marijuana. I was already reaching for the bottle to numb my pain. Why not take it a step further and really show grief how I felt about it moving in?

Benji's family and I had become detached, coping with a toxic combination of the inability to handle trauma and immeasurable sadness. None of us knew how to navigate a life with such intense loss. We were all flailing in our new realities, only being held up by each other and the numbing agents we had become so familiar with.

Christmas Eve arrived, and instead of the fancy dinner celebration we had planned, I was left with my boys. We walked through the bustling beach shops crowded with families dressed up and waiting for tables to celebrate their Christmas Eve in style, a brutal, in-your-face reminder of what we no longer had with Daddy, a complete family.

I took my boys to the nearest ice cream shop, and we found a spot on the sand to celebrate in our own way. We hadn't just lost Daddy; we had lost the strength, the stability, and the core of who we were as a family. We were forced to conjure up a new kind of family. We cuddled on the beach and anticipated a strange sort of Christmas.

The following day, I set out one gift for each boy on the balcony. They eagerly opened the video games they couldn't even play yet, and we sat silently. I felt devastated that I didn't have the energy to conjure up any more of a celebration for them. This was all I had in me.

We spent the entire Christmas day on the beach, and as I floated in the warm, shallow sea, I hummed the tune to Mele Kalikimaka and felt a tiny bit of peace. We made big sand castles, and my niece Caitlin and I took selfies in the water. We were being silly, and from the outside, no one would know this family was suffering.

God had given me a slight reprieve from my anguish. The simple Christmas morning life with Benji was on my mind but not torturous. God knew I needed to heal on an island, thousands of miles away from my old life. He knew what my heart needed to survive that day.

The first Christmas was marked off my list, but New Year's Eve followed closely behind as if all the challenging milestones were waiting in a line to torture me one by one. We explored the road to Hana on that last day of 2013. I was prepared to leave that year behind me and climb cautiously into 2014. But was I? Was I ready to let go of the last year I would have Benji? Was I prepared to move into a year he never would?

I was anticipating a possible kiss from John that night, as he had been traveling with us. But as midnight approached, I had a moment of beautiful clarity and recognized that it would have been unhealthy and unproductive on my road to healing. Everyone retreated to their rooms early that night. I left my boys in bed and walked out onto the dark beach. I could see in the corners of the beach couples snuggling, kissing, waiting to ring in a new and hope-filled year.

I sat alone on the warm sand, watching the reflections from the lit-up hotel rooms and tiki torches glowing off the crashing waves. I talked to God; I talked to Benji. I mentally prepared myself to crawl into a new year and held my breath. I counted the minutes and seconds and reluctantly crossed over into a year Benji would never see. Immediately, the new reality that Benji died last year set in. He was slowly becoming closer to my past than my future. I was living in forward motion, powerless to stop our ever-growing separation. He was staying put. He would forever remain in 2013 as I forged into an unknown future.

Returning from paradise to the freezing tundra of Salt Lake was a shock to our systems, but I was happy to be home. We jumped back into school and our new routine. Several weeks later, I left my boys with Benji's family and hopped on another plane to Florida to spend a week with my family. We rented a house just outside of Ft. Lauderdale. I noticed the alcohol drowned out my ability to heal and kept me from feeling all the hurt necessary to carry me to the other side of this loss. After several anxiety attacks and an inability to sleep, I decided to no longer use alcohol to take me through this. I wanted to feel all the pain, experience the intensity of the loss, and bring as little of it as I could into a new life. I was determined to be able to look back at my healing and know Jesus had been my sole source of real, life-giving strength, a strength I never could have received by the numbing effects of alcohol. I knew I would have to face my grief at some point; I wanted to feel it fully, get through it, and move on to the new life God had for me. I stopped drinking after that simple moment of clarity. It would take years to reform a healthy relationship with alcohol.

Shortly after Florida, I surprised my boys with a trip to Universal Studios for Valentine's Day. I told Alisha we were coming, booked the tickets, and we were on another plane a few days later. Perhaps, instead of alcohol, I was numbing with travel and escape. I had the means to leave when needed, and I was thankful for the ability. Others judged me for my inability to stay put, but I was on my own journey. I didn't let anyone's opinions of my healing process stop me.

When we were in California, Alisha and I started conversing about dating. I had now been a widow for close to six months, and I was beginning to feel that maybe, in some small way, I was ready to open my heart to someone else. I had no experience dating in this new world, and I was a jumbled-up combination of jitters and excitement about the prospects of a new love. I didn't know what it would look like, how I would go about it, and how I would include my kids, but I was confident God had a plan.

When we flew home, we had a layover in Boise. The boys and I sat in a booth waiting for our next flight, and I looked down at my shiny, platinum wedding ring, the one I had not removed in over thirteen years. I heard God's almost audible voice tell me it was time to take it off. I felt sweaty and tingly as I sat swirling in this notion, twisting the ring back and forth on my finger. I remembered the night he proposed and how the ring sat loosely on my finger. I imagined what it would feel like to present myself to the world as an unmarried woman. This concept was foreign and strange, but I was ready to conquer unknown territory. I was graduating to a different level of widowhood, a different level of existence. I was working hard at becoming unmarried.

When I arrived home, I had a moment to myself in my bedroom. I sat on the edge of the bed and pulled out the ring box with Benji's ring in it. I opened it. I looked at it. I played "Say Something" by A Great Big World and Christina Aguilera[8] and told Benji I was saying goodbye to him as my husband. I loved him. I cherished him, but I needed to be intentional about living my life unmarried to him. I cried. I sobbed. I prayed. I gave my new life to Jesus. I told Benji I was sorry I could not save him. I would have followed him anywhere, but I couldn't follow him where he went. I said goodbye to him, slipped the ring off my finger, and gently placed it in the box next to his. My ring finger had a thirteen-year-old indentation on it. A mark of love. An impact of our marriage.

The indentation could now move back to its original form, a place for my heart to be free to love again and one day be indented by someone else. I envision a closed fist. As I took my ring off, it was my way of allowing my fingers to start opening slowly. I didn't know what or who I was opening it for, but I trusted that God had a man to place into my hands. I trusted that God had a plan for my new singleness. I didn't know who would be in my future or how long I would wait, but I trusted him. He wanted me to take this first step in opening my heart.

I closed the box and placed it back on my nightstand. I stood up as a new woman, a woman free to be loved again. I was tripping over my new self, but I was simply following Benji's intentional pattern of living, and I held this moment as significant in my widow's journey—a shift in my heart, a change in my healing.

I knew the unfortunate reality; this newfound freedom in my life would not sit well with most people. I knew I would face criticism and judgment. But I pushed forward. I allowed people the space to feel awkward next to me and my ringless hand. I was willing to be open with my story. I shared my shift on my blog and allowed it to be made known. I wanted to be vulnerable and honest with my experience so they could see I was a girl following boldly after God and the new life he had waiting for me. This was not dishonoring to Benji but the opposite; healing and moving forward was the best way to honor him. If I chose to shut down and shut out life, that would oppose how Benji expressed wanting me to continue without him. This was for him.

Chapter 6
The One Where Life Started to Have Color Again

See, I am doing a new thing! Now it springs up; do you not perceive it? I am making a way in the wilderness and streams in the wasteland.
Isaiah 43:19

A Hard Journey to the Good

With each healing experience, I would feel another level of empowerment. I could look back on the past six months and see how far I had come. I had conquered hard things. My boys had endured intense hardship and could still laugh and play. God was revealing new life to us.

Six months earlier, I joined the widow club, a club that no woman ever wants to join. But with no choice of my own, I had gained a membership, a badge, and a matching t-shirt. I was a seasoned member of this crappy club.

But even though I loathed the title, God had brought new levels of healing as I clung to His strength during these long, cold months. I had survived the holidays, and even though it was still winter, I had a new hope for the coming year.

The Bible is full of stories of widows and their desperate place in society in Biblical times. They were marginalized and scrutinized. They were unable to provide for themselves in meaningful ways because the structure of society looked at them as outcasts. But God never looked at widows in that way. In fact, we have seen many times that God has a special place for widows in his heart.

In James 1:27, we read, "Religion that God our Father accepts as pure and fautless is this: to look after orphans and widows in their distress and to keep oneself polluted from the world."

Although the world around me looked at me through the glass of a fishbowl, watching my every move, God loved me with tender, loving care. I felt misunderstood by the world and saw people navigating their own grief through the lens of my actions. This felt awkward and unfair. I was thankful for God's nearness and knew He was walking me through the tumultuous waters.

On February 19th, 2014, I was sitting in front of my computer, scrolling through Facebook. A few weeks earlier, I had received a friend request from a distant friend from high school. It was one of those. Oh yeah, I remember that guy. Sure, we can be friends moments. David was the younger brother of Jimmy, a friend of Benji's and mine at our private Christian school. I remembered David as the youngest of the three boys. It had been many years since I had seen or heard from him. We had a lot of mutual friends and had most likely been at the same party or wedding at one time or another, but I did not know him.

That day, at my computer, I saw a post from David in which he shared a picture of a nice car as a way of entering a contest to win the car. It was out of character for me to comment on images shared by people I did not know well, but that day, I posted something about how if he won the car, he should take me for a ride. I was in a newfound freedom of the ability to flirt, something new and exciting for me.

We commented back and forth in the thread, and I remember thinking he would private message me at some point to keep the conversation going. At that moment, a message popped up from him asking me how old my boys were. I replied, which started days of chatting and getting to know each other. It was innocent and fun, and the thing that struck me most in those conversations was how much he made me laugh, even just through online chatting. I was drawn to him, not romantically at first, but intrigued. He was newly divorced with a child and had his own story. I knew he came from a solid Christian background and was comforted to be able to attest to his faith and character.

We chatted on and off for several weeks. David was traveling for his job, but we knew that once he returned, we would want to meet in person. On a cold Thursday afternoon, he called me on the phone, and I heard his voice for the first time. Something about him struck me again.

"The boys and I are going to a bouncy house this afternoon. Would you and Harlo want to join us?" I asked reluctantly.

"Yes, we would love to," he replied excitedly. "I have plans tonight, but I can make it work."

David had just finalized a divorce after a short marriage and had a two-year-old boy named Harlo. I wasn't hesitant about pursuing a relationship with a man with a child, as I wanted to be able to see him as a father and attest to his ability to possibly father my children someday if that is what God had planned.

As I drove to the bouncy house, I was unsure if he would make the time, but something inside me said he would. There was something that told me I was already a priority in his life, even before we had met.

I sat at a table while my boys played on the bouncy castles. I waited for David and Harlo to arrive with jitters and excitement. I was sweating and nervous. I had never met a man in hopes of a connection. My meeting with Benji was different, as we were friends in high school first. This was a new and invigorating experience.

I saw them walk in, and as David paid for the tickets, I could see Harlo's little blonde head barely sticking out over the counter. They both approached me as I got up to greet them. I wasn't sure if we would hug or shake hands, but it became a warm embrace. I noticed David was taller than I expected at a handsome 5'11", much taller than Benji, and Harlo was smaller than I expected but the most well-spoken two-year-old I had ever encountered.

After our greeting, I walked them out among the bouncy castles to meet my boys. It was a little awkward and new for all of us. Dating as parents is a new realm we had yet to navigate. We didn't know if there were right or wrong ways to go about things, but we both instantly felt comfortable including our children in our new relationship, whatever it was for now.

In our short time together that day, I told him I had recently purchased new Ikea furniture for my boys' rooms and needed help putting it together. He agreed to come over the next night, as I would pay him with pizza and beer. The next evening, he arrived with Harlo, and our boys, again, hit it off instantly. They played as we drilled and lifted and dissected the vague Ikea instructions. I was impressed at his handiness and attention to detail.

Our boys had fallen asleep in front of a movie in my bedroom, and David and I sat on my couch, talking endlessly, getting to know each other. We had yet to have a romantic spark, but we both knew we were meshing well.

The following day, I wasn't quite sure what I felt yet. But

as that Saturday afternoon went on and we communicated through text, something in my heart began to really like the man. There was something about him that made me feel seen, made me giggle, and made me see the potential.

We met at a movie theater the next day, a sunny Sunday afternoon, and took our small boys to see *The Lego Movie*. We sat in the dark, empty theater as our boys ran up and down the aisles, changing seats and wreaking quiet havoc. David and I sat close together, laughing at all the same parts, hearts pounding, the connection undeniable. I rested my hand on my leg, anticipating him to take it. After what felt like forever, with a deep breath, he reached both his hands over and cradled mine. It was electrifying and beautiful, the butterflies you only dream of.

As the day ended and we talked on the phone into the night, we agreed we should spend time together without our boys. He told me he would pick me up Thursday evening for our first official date. Our feelings grew stronger and stronger that week, and we could not wait to see each other again.

When Thursday arrived, he texted me he was on his way and again that he was only minutes away. I could hardly stand the intense feelings I was having. I opened the door to find this tall, handsome man standing with a rose, waiting to whisk me away. I jumped into his arms, and the connection was solidified. He came in and met my mom, who was there to watch the boys. He handed my mom a rose, and although I knew in her heart she was not ready to see me with another man, she pushed through with a smile.

My people were concerned for me. They didn't think I was ready for a new relationship and worried I would be hurt again. I could sense everyone's hesitation.

In my early days of grief, God held me up. His strength was being made perfect in my weakness (2 Corinthians 12:9). I felt God's courage pulsing through my veins. But I felt untrusted. I felt like people were so concerned about little ol' Heidi that she couldn't make wise decisions for her future. They held tightly to the old mantra no one should ever make big decisions in the first year after a loss. I sensed everyone viewed me as weak and fragile, but I knew I was strong, even at my most vulnerable, because of God. God had me on the fast track to new life, and I was riding along with my whole heart.

In the book of Ruth, we read about a young widow facing the decision to either stay in her old life layered with memories of loss and grief or choose God, choose an unknown new life, and choose hope. She ultimately decided to return with her mother-in-law, Naomi, to Israel and start a new life after they had both been widowed. Naomi encouraged her to stay with her people. "But Ruth said, 'Do not urge me to leave you or to return from following you. For where you go I will go, and where you lodge I will lodge. Your people shall be my people, and your God my God'" (Ruth 1:16, ESV). Ruth made the tough decision to walk into unknown territory, a new life, seeking healing and restoration.

This was terrifying for her, but she trusted God and allowed His courage to saturate her soul. This decision to stay with Naomi led to an abundant new life, more than she could have ever dreamed of. Ruth found a new husband and had a baby, and the lineage eventually led to Jesus—God's best plan in her life of loss.

Like Ruth, I clung to this promise. I could not see my future, but I could trust the one who knew where I was going.

This was a lesson in following God no matter what the world told me. Even with my family's best intentions and their love for me, God knew best. I knew all my people were hurting and could not stand by and witness me make a mess of my widowed life. I felt compassion for their broken hearts and never held their concern against them. I understood their worries. I understood their pain. We were all in this horrific nightmare together.

The road to healing was still long and perilous, but I could appreciate it at this six-month mark. I felt like if I could go through this loss and still find purpose, new life, and new love, then there was nothing I couldn't do. I was gaining a Wonder Woman complex. I felt empowered and strong, but only because of God.

After I hugged the boys goodbye, we got in the car, and

David took me to my favorite sushi restaurant. We talked and stared at each other, living in surreal moments of connection, something neither of us was ready for in our fragile states. After dinner, he walked me through the outdoor mall in downtown Salt Lake and showed me items he had built, including jewelry cases at Tiffany's and displays at Macy's. He was proud of his work and honored to introduce me to his passion for woodworking.

As we rode the escalator up to the mall's second floor, he looked down at me and kissed me. The passion was real. The connection was real, and it didn't stop there. We listened to "Magic" by Coldplay in the car as he took me home, which was exactly what it felt like. Magic.

As the weeks went on, the connection was so intense and so strong we had to, at one point, stop in our tracks and ask ourselves if this was real or just a manifestation of our losses and desires to be loved again. We were both aware of our delicate states. We were both coming out of trauma on some level. I was widowed, and he was newly divorced. This was a recipe for disaster from a worldly perspective. We were aware of the fragility of our relationship and wanted to be careful with our hearts and the hearts of our children. But we were also aware we served a big God who could be grand enough to give us a new love right out of the gate . . . a love this magnificent.

We found out later the day we started talking, February 19th, was just days after I took off my wedding ring and the exact day his divorce was final, something we were not aware of. God did not waste one single moment. We knew death and divorce were not God's desire for our lives, but we believed He could restore anything. He has the power to redeem loss and create beauty out of ashes (Isaiah 61:3). He was weaving our heartache for good, unfolding right before our eyes.

Throughout the spring and summer months, we privately relished in our new love and didn't want to spoil God's creation.

On one of our first dates, a cold March night, we sat

nestled in a warm booth in a local brewery. I rehashed the devastating story of Benji's sickness and death. I explained in vivid detail all that took place in those last desperate months of his life. I shared deep feelings and raw emotions that were still living on the surface. I didn't have to reach far to remember exactly what had happened and describe the trauma I still processed every day. He sat close to me that night, looking right at me and taking in every word. He wiped my heavy tears as his own tears flooded his sweet face. Because he had known Benji in high school, he felt the loss, too. He knew the weight of the world losing the amazing man that Benji was. David was a safe space for me to still love Benji, cherish what we had, and, with the help of God, open my heart to include David.

David was romantic and intentional about pursuing a relationship with me. On another date a few weeks later, he started to share his memories of Benji. The particular memory he shared that evening had been on his heart, but he was waiting for the right time to tell me.

In 2006, Benji and I attended a large Foursquare Church in Draper. Benji belonged to a weekly men's Bible study, where they studied a book by John Eldredge, *Wild at Heart*. It is a brilliant book that encourages men to be all they were created to be: strong, capable, God-fearing men.

David was at the same study and remembers conversing with the group about the kind of fathers they wanted to be. At the time, Jonah was a baby and our only child. David was not a father yet.

That night, as we sat in the dimly lit steak house, David told me he remembered Benji describing the kind of father he wanted to be to Jonah. He wanted to be hands-on and involved, teaching him everything he knew about being a man of God. Benji commented he had seen David's father, Jim, father them in their youth. He admired David's family and was inspired by how he was raised.

This is the moment we fully realized God had ordained this relationship, and even seven years earlier, He had started to prepare David's heart to father my boys. David didn't realize it at the time of the Bible study, but he was hearing straight from Benji's mouth how he wanted his sons to be raised, unaware he would one day be the one to raise them.

This was just one small piece of the redemption puzzle God was slowly and gracefully putting into place for our future together. God was weaving together a beautiful tapestry of goodness from the broken pieces of sickness, divorce, and loss.

God has a unique and otherworldly ability to create beauty from ashes. His hand can miraculously make order where there is chaos and bring things together no human could.

This conversation began to clarify our place with each other. We started seeing it from a heavenly perspective and knew God was doing something more significant than we could fathom.

As we spent more and more time with our three boys, we felt like we were becoming a family. Jonah and Isaac were clinging to David. They didn't understand the challenging dynamics of seeking attention and love from a man other than their daddy, but they were finding what they needed in David. David would play with them, wrestle with them, and they were slowly retrieving what they had lost when Benji died. I opened my heart more to David becoming a permanent part of our family as I watched him with Harlo. I began caring for, loving, and nurturing Harlo, just as I would want my boys to be loved and nurtured.

It was comforting that David knew Benji. He had fond memories of him in high school, and when I would speak of the man I grieved, he knew who I was talking about. This made sense to me. I never would have thought I would need a man who knew Benji and the comfort and validation I would receive from that, but God knew. God knew I would need to stay in the confines of the tight-knit community of our high school. Benji's friends knew the man David was and the family that he came from.

For some, this was uncomfortable and too close to home; to others, it made them feel safe.

As I started to reveal my relationship with David, I was sensitive to how each person would take the news and took meticulous care not to release it publicly until I had addressed the issue of my dating gently to all the people who loved Benji the most.

Benji's mother, Leonie, is a sensitive and kind woman. I took her to lunch one day to let her know that another man was in my life. I was nervous as I tried to put myself in her shoes. She was a desperately devastated mother who had lost her son. She was terrified it might mean an end to her relationship with her grandsons when I began to move forward. I have always been very aware of the complex emotions that come with a loss. I knew Benji's siblings and friends felt a certain way about me moving forward. I knew although they ultimately didn't want me to be alone, they still didn't want to see me with another man. Seeing Heidi with someone new calcified Benji's absence.

When I told Leonie I was dating David, she immediately smiled. She graciously accepted this news as she had fond memories of David and his family. She recounted years before when she was struggling to raise her four kids as a single mother. One Christmas, David's family dropped off gifts for the whole family. Although this idea of me moving forward with a new man was challenging to accept, it could not be anyone better in her eyes. David was a perfect match.

Benji's sister Erica, although reluctant, was trying her best to help me walk through the uncomfortable parts of navigating life without Benji, which, at this point, meant allowing another man to come in. We all met at a baseball game one evening, and as the awkwardness soaked in, she stood strong in her love for me and the boys, no matter how strange.

David often traveled with his job for weeks at a time. This was hard but good. It was easing us into a time where we would be together all of the time. I still had things I needed to process and firsts I needed to pass. I told David that although my love was deep and I wanted him to be a part of everything, I needed to pass the first milestones or certain holidays alone. I needed my success in the first year without Benji to be because I relied on Jesus, not because I had a man in my life.

In April, Benji's brother gifted the family an Eastern Caribbean cruise, a much-needed reprieve for all of us from the heaviness of grief. I loaded my boys on a plane once more and headed for paradise. I didn't want to leave David. I was ready to travel and live with him, but I was again alone. Alone in a stateroom with the boys, unlike everyone else without a partner on the trip. The southern sun was hot and bright, but I was agonizingly alone inside. Missing David compounded my grief. I was grieving and craving new life, all in the same breath. Joy burst through in certain moments of the trip, but it ended with me craving to return to our new little family. I was eager to get on with my new life, with David a part of it.

That summer, we purchased season passes to Lagoon, our local amusement park. We spent every Sunday afternoon playing with our boys, riding the rides, and the wings of hope we all felt as our family formed.

David and I both grew up camping. David's family would take frequent trips to Red Fish Lake in Idaho, and he wanted to share it with us. We packed up our tents and headed out for a five-day adventure. We learned a lot about each other as we navigated travel, parenting, cooking, and learning how to mesh our lives. I was forming a bond with Harlo as another mother in his life, a role I had not anticipated. This new role was just another added layer to the newness forming in my life.

I was pursuing a new life and love but was also still in transition mode in my heart. I was still, on a daily basis, in the process of undoing my life with Benji.

On May 8th, I posted on Facebook

"Received Benji's Red Butte Gardens membership card in the mail, had to cancel it, received a call asking for him, had to tell the person that he passed, had my grandma ask how Benji is feeling (she's a little forgetful), had to tell her again that he passed, had to delete Benji's name from school registration form, listened to Isaac read a whole book for the first by himself without sharing it with Benji, grilled for the first time without Benji in the backyard sipping a beer, met three babies in the last week that will never know him . . . just a few of the millions of little hurdles I have to jump that gets me closer to healing . . . getting there . . . slowly."

"I can do all this through him who gives me strength"
(Phil 4:13, NIV)

As we anticipated the July 4th holiday, the boys and I planned a trip back to Minneapolis to see our best friends, Scott and Kami, to soften the sting of celebrating another first.

Benji, the boys, and I had a significant tradition of spending the holiday with our friends Jesse and Tiffany and their daughter, Ava. Jesse was the best man at our wedding, and we cherished the deep friendships we had created over the years of building our families. They would come to our house every year, and we would grill some delicious summer food. Tiffany would make her famous margaritas. We would set up water toys in the backyard, pump up the summertime tunes, and soak in the perfect Utah summer air. Benji and Jesse would risk their lives lighting fireworks in the street as Tiffany and I would hold our little ones close, ears covered and wrapped in blankets. The first July 4th without this tradition was brutal for all of us. Grief hung thick and heavy that Independence Day.

As we were celebrating and trying to create new

memories in Minnesota, my heart craved the old, regular life that made sense. We watched fireworks over the Mississippi River; I took in the loss, acknowledged what it once was, and embraced the new. I didn't know what each celebration of America would look like in my life going forward, and I was powerless to stop the steep climb to a new normal. However, I wasn't only lamenting. I was surrounded by friends who were championing me on my journey, and I knew David was waiting for me at home.

It was odd and uncomfortable for my friends to accept I had a new man in my life, but as we talked about it, Scott said, "It will be weird until it's not weird." I was thankful they were willing to walk with me through the crazy, awkward roads to my new life.

Dating as a parent comes with many loaded and unexpected dynamics to sift through. I strove to weave through grieving Benji while simultaneously creating a place for David in my heart. And with him, I had to make a place for Harlo and, unexpectedly, his mother.

One thing I didn't fully process when I started dating a divorced dad was that that child would have a mother. The enemy took root in my heart, and a spirit of jealousy took over. I fell madly in love with this man, but he had a past. He had been in love before. He had been married before. Another woman used to be his everything, and they shared a child. I began to compare myself to her and question why he would love me over her. I asked why I was different. I started to live in fear he would decide to go back to her and leave me in the dust. These thoughts taunted me as I learned to walk out of this new life. I began to be needy and suspicious and was forced to deal with emotions that were foreign to me.

I never dealt with jealousy with Benji. We dated young, married young, and never had to process our lives before we were together. There was never another woman. This was all new territory for me. David's gracious heart gently walked me through all my misconceptions and misunderstandings about their divorced relationship. He calmed my fears and held me close as I navigated this uncomfortable territory.

After arriving home from the July 4th trip to Minneapolis, David picked me up from the airport, and we headed out to meet Harlo's mom, Kelci, to do a switch. I was sweaty and nervous about meeting the girl who mothered David's son. We both got out of the car and walked hesitantly towards one another. We shook hands and introduced ourselves. Both of us were unfamiliar with this type of relationship. We needed to figure out who we were to each other. This meeting began a journey of a relationship like none I had before. We had to navigate sharing a man but in different ways. David struggled with having two women in his life but playing different roles. This complex dynamic took intentionality, thoughtfulness, and loads of grace. I had to make space for her in my life if I was going to be with David. I had to accept his past and not allow it to swallow me whole.

During this time, the boys and I were still steadily going to therapy. I was able to gush out all my feelings and thoughts on grieving, the boys grieving, dating with kids, processing another woman amid our relationship, and all that comes with that. Sara, my therapist, was gracious and patient with me as I trekked through so many unfamiliar and complex emotions. The boys continued to move forward in their healing, and I was always on high alert as they were also hiking through unknown trails of loss that didn't make any sense. I was conscious of their reactions to David and wanted to be sensitive to anything they felt was uncomfortable.

Nick had been living with us since November. Filling the man void in our home that had been left empty when Benji died. Nick held me up in the first months of widowhood, but it was his time to move on. He accepted a job in Denver, and in late July, we said goodbye. The boys and I stood in the driveway on a hot summer evening just as the sun was setting. We hugged and cried with Uncle Nick. I have a photo of the three of them red-faced and smiling through their tears. Nick had been the rock we needed, but it was time for David to step in as the strong male in their life. God's timing baffled me. It is so delicate, intricate, and perfect. Watching for God in painful moments eases the sting as we trust He is doing the best for us, even when it hurts.

In this moment, I found myself not only missing life with Benji but also missing when life made sense. Our family made sense—mom, dad, and kids. We didn't have complex relationships to sift through or unusual dynamics to process. But even with those complicated feelings swirling around me, I still felt an excitement for what was to come.

Benji's "would be" 34th birthday was at the end of July, and his family, friends, and I felt it appropriate to celebrate big, even without him here. We gathered all his favorite people, ate his favorite food, played his favorite music, and drank his favorite beer. We laughed, and we cried. We played "Wish You Were Here" by Pink Floyd while holding green and blue balloons in the backyard. We let the balloons go as the music blasted through the warm summer air. Benji left a gaping hole in our lives, and we were standing together, facing the dilemma, recognizing how much he was missing. We allowed ourselves the space to meet the pain and feel the hurt but also acknowledged his presence in our lives, which only made us better people.

As each milestone passed, the one-year mark was bitterly taunting me. In his final days, Benji said I needed to get through the first year. After that, I would be okay; all would be well. I took this to heart and planned another Disneyland trip with Scott and Kami to celebrate one year of grief. One year of survival. We planned to be in Disneyland on September 7th, the death-aversary. I knew I needed a real distraction even to be able to breathe that day.

The morning of our trip, I dropped the boys off at school and had the unbelievable urge to visit the cemetery. I was craving Benji's presence. I had enormous mountains of things to tell him—all he had missed in the last year, things the boys did and said, and about David. I needed him to know I was ok.

I drove to the cemetery, unable to get there fast enough. I wove through the traffic, my tear-filled eyes striving to see clearly. I pulled up to the manicured place where my husband was buried and threw myself on his gravestone. The pain welled up. The tears flowed. My words slurred.

I wished more than anything I could hear his voice. I craved his calming presence to ease my hurting heart. I ached to tell him everything and how I had lived one year without him. I had journeyed through every milestone, every holiday, every ugly, lonely day of being his widow. I wanted him to know it all. Some would say, in their most compassionate intentions, that he knows. However, that notion was never comforting to me; it doesn't make me feel better that he might see how the boys have grown.

I wanted to experience it with him.

I wanted him here.

I didn't just want him to know; I wanted him to experience it, to live it with me.

We went to Disneyland to celebrate one year of my accomplishment while also acknowledging that the world was Benji-less for one year. We enjoyed Disneyland and ended the seventh while watching the World Of Color. I was void of emotion. I didn't cry. I didn't weep. I just was. There are so many expectations humans put on grief: When we should cry. When we should lament. When it's okay to laugh or smile. Sometimes, I would feel guilty for certain feelings or the lack thereof. I was living the only widow life I knew how. I learned over time it is a personal process. I can't put expectations on any day, milestone, or any emotion or lack thereof. It simply is what it is.

I landed home as an official one-year widowed woman. I felt liberated. I felt a new sense of freedom. I had surpassed every "first" with God by my side. I had been given David, who helped me when appropriate, but I had done it. I had done the hard things. I could take a deep breath and prepare to move forward with my new life with David. I was not naive. I knew I had more to grieve, heal, and move past, but I allowed myself to sit and rest in the space of the one-year mark. I had heard that year two was the hardest, but I let myself feel the accomplishment of making it one year without him. Benji would have said in his proudest voice, "You did it!"

Chapter 7
The One Where I Got Remarried

"To be loved but not known is comforting but superficial. To be known and not loved is our greatest fear. But to be fully known and truly loved is, well, a lot like being loved by God."
Timothy Keller[9]

A Hard Journey to the Good

In October, David and I met with the pastor of David's church to seek advice for our quickly advancing relationship.

Chad did not hesitate when he boldly told us we should marry because of our delicate situation and the involvement of three precious souls if we felt God calling us together. There was no reason to prolong the inevitable. Our boys needed consistency and stability.

We sat in the car after the meeting, and I felt anxious and overwhelmed by the notion of getting married again. I was positive this was God's plan, but it was heavy. God's plan for the redemption of my life was full speed ahead, but I trusted Him. I trusted His perfect timing.

We knew that since we had been essentially keeping our relationship in the shadows, releasing the information, with the added bonus of an engagement, meant we were in for a treat as far as judgment went. We began slowly telling those closest to us about our plans to marry. Our closest friends and family all knew David was in my life, but they were not yet aware of the seriousness of our relationship. We had a mix of reactions. Those that weren't as close to us were thrilled. They could clearly see two people from hurtful pasts find love again. It was a beautiful thing to be celebrated.

The other half, those closest to me, pummeled me with unacceptance of this choice. I was told I should not marry a divorced man. I was told it was too soon. I was accused of moving forward faster than anyone was ready. They could not begin to grasp the notion I could love two men. In their fragile and grieving hearts, they only saw that if I loved and invited another man into my life, I would have to shove Benji out. There would be no room.

These words were offensive and hurtful on every level. In my blog, I put up my dukes and began to fiercely defend myself, explaining that just like our hearts expand when we have a second child, a widow's heart can grow to love a new man while simultaneously continuing to love her late husband. It is a balancing act, but somehow, by the grace of God, I was pulling it off. Loving two men.

Some believed David was manipulating me, trying to keep our relationship a secret. But the truth was far more tender—we chose to keep things quiet out of respect for those who loved Benji most. I wasn't trying to hide my new life; I was trying to protect others from unnecessary pain. As a widow, I had the sacred opportunity to make space in my heart for a new husband. But for a grieving mother or a sibling, finding room for someone new—another son, another brother—is different. That kind of space isn't easily made or even always possible. My loss, as painful as it was, allowed for a kind of rebuilding. Their loss did not offer the same kind of room. It was a different kind of grief. My path forward looked different because my loss held a different shape.

I was sensitive to these notions and could feel their resentment, and I did my best to welcome their discomfort. This is not to say my heart wasn't pained by the judgment. I felt the unfairness that a widow not only grieves but has to live her life defending her healing. I hashed it out in therapy and learned the art of grace. I hoped and prayed that one glorious day, they could see the hand of God in this story and that they, too, could learn to love David.

Thanksgiving approached, and so did the upcoming awkwardness I knew would be mine when I received an invitation for dinner at Benji's family's home. In years past, Benji, the boys, and I would split our time between my family and his. I asked Benji's family if I could bring David to join us for Thanksgiving dinner, and the answer was no. As I look back, I don't condemn them for this choice, and I can brutally understand walking into that home with another man would have been uncomfortable on levels none of us were ready for. It had been fourteen months since Benji left the earth. The pain was still acute. The grief was still abounding, and hearts were not ready for new steps into a new life for them or me.

I was able to wrap my head around my new life much sooner than most of those around me. I began grieving Benji long before he took his last breath. The loss was gradual. The grief was anticipatory. Others still had Benji when he was sick on a less intense level. He was still alive. They could text, hang, chat, and be involved in each other's lives in a normal way.

That was not the case for our relationship. Our home was different. I experienced loss in small, consequential ways in my everyday life. We lost the intimacy of husband and wife early on when I took on the role of caregiver. I saw our home life disintegrate. I witnessed it melting right before my eyes. I was alone long before he left. I was a single parent months before his passing, and I began grieving the man I married the day he was diagnosed.

Soon after his devastating end-of-life prognosis, Benji rested in the living room, and the boys and I played in their room. I recognized, at that moment, the separation was happening. It was him . . . and then us. Because of these early losses, I was prepared and ready to move forward much sooner than anyone else. This created a rift in what once were strong relationships. We grieved at different paces. I was miles ahead. So when it was time for my heart to be opened, they were just coming to terms with the fact he was gone. When I was ready to make choices to build a new life, they had just noticed the casket was closed.

Unfortunately, this left me feeling scrutinized and judged.

The tears streamed as we prepared dinner for the first Thanksgiving with David and my family. I understood Benji's family's hearts, but I had to stand firm. I wasn't going there without David.

They asked if only Jonah and Isaac could join them for dinner, and we started coordinating a gas station exchange. However, I realized this was beginning to feel like a divorce. Benji and I did not get divorced. I would not allow my children to feel like they were being exchanged in hostility.

My heart hurt for myself, my heart broke for my boys, and my heart ached for the family. The rebuilding of my own life was divisive and ugly. It tore at all of us. I kept circling back to going to their dinner to calm the storm, even for a little while, but my mom was my strength.

She was adamant she would not let us go. She refused to see me walk into a home full of people with animosity towards me and my life choices. She couldn't stomach seeing her daughter in such a tormenting setting after everything I had been through.

After much pleading, long text messages, and hostile phone conversations, I boldly told them we would not join them. End of story. That year, I missed Thanksgiving with the Edmunds for the first time in sixteen years. I explained we were a package deal: me, the boys, and David. This was my new family, and we would not be separated to appease any awkwardness. This may have lacked compassion, but I had to place boundaries around my new family.

I hung up the phone and slipped off my parents' bed into a ball on the floor. Emotions took over, and I sobbed in the tearing, the pulling, and the gnawing of my journey to find newness. I did not want to hurt anyone. I just wanted to find redemption from my loss. The only thing I was doing was creating a new life for the boys and me. I felt ridiculed and judged beyond anything I felt before.

But I trusted God was in this storm. This was not a surprise to Him. He knew the hearts that were hurting. He was working on each of us individually and pulling us towards healing, as painful as it was.

David sat on the floor, holding me as I rocked in sorrow. He could see the brutality of starting over with him but chose to stay. He decided to be involved. He chose to be the new guy. He chose me.

After my bold decline of their dinner invitation, I began to receive text messages of remorse over their treatment of me. They started apologizing, begging us to join them, but I stood firm. I told them no. I wept through dinner with my family and ended the day feeling depleted and heartbroken but accomplished for standing my ground. I was learning to follow God's direction for us without compromise.

This incident was a catalyst for healing for our entire

family. My boldness in remaining firm in my new life and the inclusion of David forced them to quickly realize if they didn't begin to allow their hearts to be open to a new man in my life, they would also lose me and the boys. They eventually came to recognize that their resentment toward me moving forward was creating distance between us. That realization softened their hearts, and from there, we began a bumpy, but sincere journey toward reconciliation.

On December 1st, David, the three boys, and I were watching a movie at David's home. We could hear the boys arguing in the other room, and David checked the situation. He called for me, asking for my intervention. I was slightly annoyed he couldn't handle the scuffle alone, but I went in to see what was happening. The boys were on the top bunk fighting over a small item. I asked them what was worth all the fuss, and with a sneaky smile, Jonah handed me a shiny diamond ring. I turned to David just as he got down on one knee.

In his nervous and sweet voice, he said, "Heidi, will you marry me?"

I was taken aback and surprised, but with a complete and confident heart, I shouted, "Yes!"

The boys cheered. David and I hugged with tears of thankfulness. We had found our new home with each other. We followed God bravely beyond our tragedies and stepped into a new adventure with each other and our sweet boys.

We sat on his couch and took cuddly selfies of our giddy faces and my stunning ring, jeweled with pink sapphires, sitting around a shiny diamond. We boldly posted our engagement on Facebook as the congratulations poured in. Friends from high school, people who knew both of us and had watched loss unfold as Benji left us, could now witness God's goodness on display. Their acceptance, excitement, and approval spurred us in our quest for life with each other. We were solid in our commitment to this new brave road, not knowing what it would look like or where it would take us. We envisioned a life with each other, passionate about serving God in significant ways. This news was still difficult for those closest to me, and I navigated it delicately.

The word courage appears thirty times in the Bible. In Mark 6:50, Jesus' disciples are afraid after seeing Him walk on water, but Jesus encourages them to trust Him. God speaks of courage to Joshua as he leads the Israelites to Canaan, and in Psalms 27:14, the writer encourages us to be brave.

God understands we live in a shaky world. He does not expect us just to grin and bear it to make it through. We are not responsible for manifesting our desires and hoping things work out. He graciously has a plan and strengthens us to take bold steps.

In Deuteronomy 33:27, we read, "The eternal God is your refuge, and underneath are the everlasting arms." When we trust God and follow Him into unknown territory, we can walk securely, knowing we are safe in His arms. We can dare to be bold because God is our refuge.

By saying yes to David, I was saying yes to God; He was asking me to bravely take a step into a new marriage, which was exciting and scary all at the same time. I was nervous but also felt so blessed. I would fight against fear as I knew I was possibly setting myself up for more loss if something ever happened to David. Staying single and never opening my heart again would be more comfortable. I could live the rest of my life alone, knowing I would never be widowed again. However, I was young, my boys needed a father in their lives, and I knew God brought us together. God infused in me great courage to step into a new adventure with David despite my fears of the unknown.

As Christmas approached, we began to plan our wedding and chose January 31st, 2015, as our wedding date. I had little desire for a big to-do. I simply wanted to become David's wife. Because of the looming animosity from some close friends and family, we decided our wedding would only include our parents and siblings. This left no room for hurt feelings. We would not invite anyone who would not want to be there, and we were not including some to leave out others. We decided to have the cut-off with immediate family only. This created a simplicity in the planning and a light-hearted and easy feel as our wedding day approached. Although we left some hurt feelings in the wake, we trusted this was the best way to celebrate our marriage. It was not my job to make everyone feel comfortable; I had to keep moving forward.

We were excited to be enjoying our first Christmas season together, and even though we were not living together yet, we enjoyed all the festivities for our new little family. I felt my love for Christmas reignite as I felt hope for our future and could see past my deep grief. I was thankful that I only had to spend one holiday season alone. David was a perfect new partner, and it was exciting to build new traditions.

Benji and I had always had an artificial tree. We purchased a plastic tree on clearance the year before we were married. It was always such a challenge putting it up. The branches had to be put in place individually, and every year, I would spend a whole hour fluffing out the needles. I sold the tree that first year without Benji. It was another small part of saying goodbye to that life. David and I started the tradition of perusing the tree lots and picking out the perfect real tree. We decorated our living tree with tinsel and lights and took a photo of the three boys standing in front of the new tree, another anchor in the creation of our new family.

Just a week before Christmas, my sister Chelsea had her first baby, little River Rose. Her arrival was a blessing for our family as we had lost so much, but she added to the joy of welcoming David and Harlo into our family. It was precious to welcome that sweet girl into my life. She lit me up and always will. She was just another sign of new life and the goodness of God our family so desperately needed.

On Christmas Eve, the boys and I spent time with Benji's family, and we traditionally did dinner and presents that day. No one was ready for David to join, so we went without him. Even as they were slowly coming around to the idea of him, they were still not ready to include him in family functions. A bit of healing and acceptance had started to emerge, so I felt safe attending. This felt different than Thanksgiving because they began to accept David in other ways. It was a conscious choice for David and I to go our separate ways that Christmas Eve, the last one we would spend apart.

However, I felt a pull from the Edmund family that day. They will forever be my family, but the dynamic was changing. My life was morphing, creating a different space for them. I had hoped one day, they would have a new and permanent place, but I was still determining where that was and what it would look like. I was unsettled in the newness, as I am sure they were too. How were they supposed to let another man who was not Benji into their homes? I didn't know the answer and sat with them in the uncomfortable questions. We were all still grappling with the weight of our loss and the inevitable, complex changes it brought to every part of our lives. The boys and I enjoyed our time as much as possible and left to meet David.

While we were at the Edmunds, David had gone to help with something at Kelci and Harlo's apartment. While there, he was faced head-on with losing his marriage to Kelci and the life they created together. He felt the tension of the life he chose to leave and the life he was now choosing. As he was being pulled towards a new life and family, he wondered what the new dynamic would be.

We both sat together in similar but different spaces in our hearts. We were building a new life, forcing us to let go of old things, people, and ways of life. We were tearing down and building up all in the same breath. We were starting our life together while simultaneously letting go of our old lives. We weren't saying goodbye to the old permanently. It was all just taking up a different space in our lives.

God was infusing us with the bravery to take on new things, morphing our lives, in hopes He had something new and fabulous for us on the other side.

On Christmas morning, after we had finished opening presents, Jonah escaped into his room. He returned with a small gift for David: the measuring tape, the small trinket he had purchased at school that read, "My Dad Rules." When he chose that toy the year before, only weeks after Benji passed, he had high hopes of giving it to a new daddy. He did not know his new daddy would be a carpenter, and a tape measure would surely come in handy.

Jonah handed it to David with a small smile, and David's eyes lit up as soft tears fell. This was another precious confirmation we were all on the path to healing.

New Year's Eve was yet another contrast to the previous year. Instead of spending it alone on a beach, David and I snuggled on the couch as the boys slept. We rang in the new year. It was a new, exciting year of our marriage and an unknown journey ahead.

As 2015 started, we began transforming my home as David and Harlo prepared to move in. We knew it would be uncomfortable and awkward, but we were comforted by the idea it would be temporary. I had lived with Benji in that house for nine years. It would be strange to have David move in, but that was the best we could do then.

We hoped God had a plan and a new space for us. As I helped clean out and pack up David's home in preparation to sell, I was again bombarded with the reality that Kelci was once his wife. David was sifting through drawers and baskets of things that belonged to her. I was curious about their short time together but also couldn't stand the idea. I was stepping in places I didn't belong and looked forward to a time when he was with me longer than he was with her. He needed to sift through that life and clear it out. I helped him some but left it up to him to remove her even more from his life as his wife. We finally cleared it out, put the home on the market, and sold it. We took carloads to my house and placed moving boxes into my basement.

We rearranged the bedrooms and had to get creative to

make room for two more people to live in our small home. There were two bedrooms on the main level, and we decided to give the three boys the master bedroom because it was bigger. We crammed in two bunk beds end to end and created a fun kid space.

We purchased a new king-sized mattress, hoping it would fit into our own home one day. But for the time being, we squeezed it into the small second bedroom. It nearly took up the entire thing, with barely enough room to walk on each side with the large dressers lined up against one wall. We didn't have a bed frame yet, so the mattress sat on the floor—humble beginnings for our new life.

January sped by as we planned our small celebration. I purchased a dress from a clearance rack at Nordstrom. The dress was a pale pink, knee-length, with a sheer flowing bottom and the top covered in silk, rose-shaped details. It was a sleeveless, informal, and unique dress for a wedding. I was aiming to have a purely simple wedding. I had grown and matured past my obsession with the perfect wedding from fifteen years before. I was a different person. I had experienced life and had learned for myself what was necessary. We had a small budget, so we planned to do all the decorations ourselves. We ordered one hundred white roses from Costco, and I created small centerpieces for a large "U" shaped table for our two families to enjoy our wedding dinner. I purchased inexpensive vases and decor from Ikea and made it our own.

We chose a quaint log cabin restaurant up in the mountains for the location, just a short drive from home in the city. Our wedding took place in the depths of winter, and the log cabin was surrounded by deep snow and frozen waterfalls. We chose the small library for our ceremony and formal dinner. The restaurant party planner gave us liberty with the small space to do as we wanted.

During our engagement, I struggled with an overwhelming amount of guilt—guilt I was living, guilt I was happy, guilt there would be another man in the boys' life. I felt the enemy try to bombard me with the fear that getting remarried was a mistake, and it would end disastrously. But I knew, without a doubt, what God spoke to us about getting married. It was undeniable. I knew I was supposed to marry David and walk into the unknown on his arm.

I fought through the lies and the fear and kept planning. Getting remarried as a widow is a complicated ocean of emotions. It is not the easy, lovely excitement of a first-time bride. My experience was layered with all the hard things of my past, David's past, and the lives and well-being of our children, questioning whether I would be able to handle the arduous life of a remarried widow/stepmom. Watching Benji take his last breath and saying goodbye to my best friend was gut-wrenchingly hard, but having to keep living was harder.

The night before our wedding, we invited David's family to my parents' house, where the families could finally meet. We had pizza and beer, opened gifts, and allowed a space for our families to be united before the wedding. David decorated our small, white, layered cake with white roses, and Chelsea helped me build my bouquet using YouTube video instructions.

The next day, before heading up the mountain to the wedding venue, all the girls gathered at the blowout bar near my home—the same place my sisters and I had visited before Benji's funeral. But this time, the occasion was different. This time, I could tell the stylist I was getting married, not preparing to bury my husband. The shift in tone was striking, yet the conversation still carried an undercurrent of heaviness. When she asked the simple question, "How did you two meet?" it landed like a stone. I offered a condensed version of a story that was anything but simple, and I could see in her eyes that she hadn't been expecting such weight in such a casual moment.

We all got our hair done and enjoyed getting to know each other. I was excited to have a new mother-in-law, two new sisters, and two new nieces. As I sat in the chair, David, his brother, and Dad popped by to give us a bottle of wine to enjoy as we got ready. David stayed in the car to not see his bride before the wedding. Jim handed me the bottle of wine with such a look of joy and excitement on his face. At that moment, I realized this wasn't just a wedding; it was a significant event proving God can truly work anything for good. Death and divorce did not have the final say.

After we were all pampered and beautiful, we headed to the cabin to decorate. We created an intimate space with small candles lining the library shelves and mantels. We set tiny vases with white roses, displayed the centerpieces, and decorated a table for our sand ceremony.

After the preparations were ready, we retreated to the bride's room. I slipped into my dress, finalized my make-up and jewelry, and jittered in the nervous excitement that David and I were going to be man and wife.

I heard a slight knock at the door as soon as I was ready. I opened the door and saw my sweet little men standing with big grins, thrilled for what would happen. I knelt to them, explaining how God had brought many new and unique people into our lives, people who love God and love us. God had planned a new journey for us, restoring what the locusts had eaten when Benji died. This didn't mean we were done missing Daddy. This didn't mean he wouldn't always be their number one daddy, but God was busy restoring our hearts with new love and a new journey. We still had a long, rocky path of healing ahead of us, but we would now have a new family to help us walk through it.

I took their tiny hands, and we walked around the corner into the small room where the ceremony would take place. We didn't have chairs, so our family stood around the small altar we created in front of the fireplace. The boys and I walked towards David and Harlo with a violin and guitar version of "Magic" by Coldplay playing.

A Hard Journey to the Good

There was not a dry eye in the place as everyone witnessed the coming together of two broken lives, making one new, beautiful family. The pastor spoke life and healing over us, directing us to look to God as our light and guide in the challenging blended family life. We were reminded to never lose sight of what God had created and how God wanted to use us, even when it would get hard. When the pastor asked David and me to hold hands, the boys took each other's hands. We giggled at their innocence and recognized this was not just a union of us but a union of them.

David and I read our vows aloud to each other. David mentioned Benji and promised the boys he would be everything they needed in a father. I vowed to love him and Harlo with all of my heart. We promised to keep God in the center of our marriage and vowed to love each other through all the challenges that were sure to be ours.

After our vows, we stepped over to the small table with five jars of sand, each a different color. We spent time each pouring our sand into one jar. This ceremony symbolized the blending of our family and how nothing could separate us. The table was lined with black, white, purple, orange, and red sand jars, a forever symbol of God's provision and blessing on our new family.

After our I do's, a prayer, and the first announcement of our union, we shared our first kiss, and "Brown Eyed Girl" played in the background. We signed our marriage license as our families smiled, cried, laughed, and embraced the beautiful goodness. I felt adored by David's parents as they embraced me as their baby boy's wife.

We then retreated into the blustery cold for wedding photos, and our talented photographer perfectly captured our joy.

We spent the evening in the warm library surrounded by dim candles, delicious food, and, eventually, dancing and cake. My brother Nick provided the romantic and celebratory mood with the music. We chose only a few wedding traditions that made sense. We cut the cake and had our first dance. I danced with my dad, and David danced with his mom. Our two small families danced the night away and celebrated our union. It was stunning, perfect, and everything we had hoped for.

We arranged for a driver to pick us up and take us to Park City for a small honeymoon. We stayed at a beautiful mountain resort and spent two days together in the beauty of winter as husband and wife. It felt complete to be married to David. I was far from done in my grief process, but now David was a solid part of my healing journey.

Chapter 8
The One When a Family Was Born

"'For I know the plans I have for you,' declares the LORD, 'plans to prosper you and not to harm you, plans to give you hope and a future.'"
Jeremiah 29:11

A Hard Journey to the Good

A Hard Journey to the Good

I couldn't believe I was now David's wife. We were married and had so much hope for our future, whatever it held. We arrived home from our small getaway and jumped right into family life. My boys went to school, David worked his construction job, and I stayed home. Harlo was on a back-and-forth schedule and spent his days at daycare. It was an unusual dynamic for me to have another child but only have him with us half the time. I maintained a healthy relationship with Harlo's mom, although we were still getting used to each other.

David and I took our honeymoon on a mission trip to Guatemala in February. Our church was taking a group of people with an organization called Juvenet. They did life-changing work, and we were excited to be a part of it. The timing was perfect for us to join them while celebrating our marriage. They had booked us the "honeymoon" suite at a quaint resort in Chimaltenango. It was rustic, small, and located at the top of the resort.

Although it didn't have any hot water, we were able to laugh about it as we were enthralled in our new life as husband and wife. We spent our days serving disabled orphans, delivering food to needy families, and helping serve in local churches. The most astonishing task we were given was building a house for a local widow. We spent two full days pouring concrete, building walls and furniture, and inviting in the widow and her two children. To spend time loving on and encouraging another widow was beyond meaningful. She was gracious and thankful, and I was able to pray with her. I was landing in a place in my healing that allowed me to reach out and help another grieving widow. I could use the bravery and courage God had infused into me and pour it onto someone else.

The next day, I was asked to speak at the local church with a translator and to share my story of God's goodness since losing my husband. I stood on the stage with David as I slowly recounted my story. I explained how just one year earlier to the day was the day David and I started chatting online. God carried us so far in just one short year. Redemption was evident in our lives, and it encouraged others to know God cares deeply about our losses, hurts, and struggles. He longs to bring redemption and healing to all parts of our story. At that moment, I felt complete. I knew God wasn't done with us, but it felt full circle. I could see the delicate hand of God moving through the deep valleys of pain and loss. I could see him redeem my loss in a way I could look back and see the puzzle pieces of grief begin to come together.

The congregation in that small Guatemalan church was amazed at our story, and I now had a story worth sharing that could help people and encourage others in their losses and pains. This began a many-year process as I contemplated writing a book. I wasn't ready yet as I sensed a lot more was coming, but the ideas started brewing, and I began to pray about one day getting to a place where I could share all that God had done. I wish I could have told Benji about the miraculous occurrences in my healing. I was still missing him. I was still a widow. I was still grieving, but now I had a new life and husband to help me process the trauma at a deeper level. I felt safe. Parts of it were awkward. Parts of it were better left unsaid, but David was supportive in all the ways he could be. He was not the end of my story but the beginning of a new chapter.

There were times before Benji died when I looked around and realized I had never been truly tested in my faith. I had never experienced a life-shattering incident that forced me to question the goodness of God. I had never lived through something that tore at my soul and stripped me to nothing with only one hand clinging tightly to God. I didn't wish for hardship; I just wished for an adventure.

Benji was progressing quickly in his career, and I was hopeful he would be offered a position out of state or out of the country. I would have said yes to this faster than his lips could form a sentence asking if I would like to move. Several opportunities would have landed us in the Bay Area, Boston, Seattle, or Austin, and with each possible scenario to move, I quickly jumped online and started researching life in another city. I would scour through homes, schools, and everything else a new city could offer. I desperately tried to manifest a new life somewhere else and had trouble finding contentment in the blessed life Benji, and I had in Salt Lake.

When the opportunity wouldn't pan out, I would be left devastated and clamoring to begin the journey to contentment where we were. I was hyper-aware of my discontentment and prayed God would cover me in His joy. I would recite King David's words in Psalms 16:6-8: "The boundary lines have fallen for me in pleasant places; surely I have a delightful inheritance. I will praise the LORD, who counsels me; even at night, my heart instructs me. I keep my eyes always on the LORD. With him at my right hand, I will not be shaken."

While striving to find contentment in our beautiful home, I still longed for change. I longed for adventure, but I knew God's plan was best. His ideas about my life trumped anything I could ever conjure in my head. Even if I spent countless hours planning a perfect life, adventure, and new place, I would never come close to God's best for me. So often, our humanness wants to take over. It is not easy to surrender our ideas or desires to God, but when we lay them at the feet of Jesus, He cradles our most intimate wants. He created us, and He knows us. He knows our deepest longings. When we live a life at the feet of Jesus and are willing to allow God to shape our hopes and dreams, He does more than we could ever create in our minds.

A part of me wanted to experience something to stretch my faith so I could give an account of my testimony. However, I would have never asked for such intense loss to be the thing to strengthen my faith. I wanted to allow for a space in my life for change or challenge so I could have something to encourage people with. But not this.

When I had joined the MOPS group many years before, I sat around a table of Jesus-loving mamas made up of locals and transplants from other states. Our home and church were located just below the University of Utah campus, which holds an elite medical school. Capital Church was filled with medical interns, soon-to-be doctors, and their wives. These were people who were from all over the country, living a life of adventure. I would listen to stories of how God had called them to move, stretch, and see other parts of the world. These stories only deepened my desire for adventure.

But I trusted that God knew best. Ephesians 3:20 says, "Now to him who can do far more abundantly than all that we ask or think, according to the power at work within us" (ESV).

Paul is explaining here that our Father loves us lavishly. He sent His only son to rescue us from our sins, knowing we could never earn it alone. Jesus gifted us with eternal life if we follow Him and live a life glorifying His name. God is calling us to be rooted where He has us. We can live simultaneously with longings and contentment. Both are possible.

During these years, I trusted God but longed for more. At that point, I didn't realize that God already had a plan in the works. However, the change I longed for included Benji. He was my dream partner. He was by my side in everything I had created in my head about our life of adventure. But God had other plans.

I didn't understand why Benji was called home early and why I was left to navigate building a life without him.

The unfairness nearly choked me out. I didn't understand, but I trusted God. I trusted He would redeem my life, restore my desires, and eventually, I would land in a new life with new dreams . . . an abundant new life.

At this point in my loss journey, I could see why God never allowed us to leave Utah. I needed to be right there, close to family, engulfed in our church community, and surrounded by the people who would cradle my broken heart. God knew. I could see why His answer was always no when I pleaded for an adventure.

When David and I arrived home from our mission trip, we faced an indescribable challenge that rocked us to our core. Kelci, Harlos's mom, decided she wanted to move to Washington State. She had a new relationship worth exploring and wanted a fresh start.

Before I came along, David and Kelci often talked about moving to the Pacific Northwest. After they divorced, she met Tyler, a Washington native, and David agreed he could also move for Harlo and was willing to relocate with them. He was not heavily tied to Utah and thought a fresh start would be good for him as well.

When I came along, I put a huge wedge in their plan. I was in no place to move, far from it. I always craved an adventure, but this was certainly different from how I wanted to get the opportunity to move away. I was unsettled by the idea of following David's ex-wife and didn't want her picking where we would live.

Oddly enough, Washington State was the one place Benji and I talked about moving to the most. It was the place I felt most at home. We loved the city's lush, green landscape and were not turned off by the frequency of rain. There were many tech jobs in Seattle, so if Benji and I had truly pursued moving, it likely would have been to Washington. In some small part of my heart, I always felt I would live in Washington State.

This notion of moving to Washington excited me, but I needed to prepare for that type of change. I needed time to settle into a new marriage, the boys needed more healing near their family, and we were not ready to take another leap out of our familiar way of life. We had just been bombarded with the loss of Benji. We had just welcomed David into our lives. We were not ready to say goodbye to the rest of our people.

In March, Kelci and Harlo moved to Washington. She had high hopes we would eventually join her, but this was devastating for David, me, and our boys, who had just gained a new brother. I put on a happy face to support her in her new life. I knew I wasn't the only one looking for redemption and newness. We agreed that for the time being, until we figured out our plan, Harlo would fly back and forth as much as possible. He was only three years old, but we were determined to make it work.

I was torn up. I couldn't imagine Harlo living away from David, and I felt like if I moved, I would be sacrificing the well-being of my still-grieving young boys. I could not take them from everything they had ever known. I could not move them away from the family they so desperately needed. I began to form a wave of anger with God as I could not and almost refused to believe this was part of His plan. Everything, up until this point, made a little bit of sense. This did not, and I was despondent over the situation.

After they moved, David and I took a short trip to Gig

Harbor, a small coastal town in the South Sound, to see where Kelci and Harlo lived. I had never heard of Gig Harbor before and was curious to see what it was like. We flew to Seattle and made the forty-five-minute drive down to visit their new home.

They rented a small apartment in the harbor, and we saw where Harlo was going to school.
Although the place was stunningly beautiful, God blinded me to the charm of living in the Pacific Northwest, where I had always desired to live. He didn't want us to make a rushed decision.

Before we left, we spent time driving through the tree-lined, winding streets and lush forests, looking for homes for sale in Gig Harbor. David was excited and ready to make the big move. I tried to be excited but knew what awaited me at home: two boys who needed consistency and stability, not an out-of-state move. I needed my family, and Benji's family would never support this. I had a house I wasn't ready to sell and a community of friends I could not see myself living without. I needed to prepare. All the odds were stacked against this happening.

When we arrived home, David was ready to start interviewing for jobs and continuing the research of homes and schools. We had not been married for two months and were already on entirely different pages of how our future would look. It was disheartening and confusing. I could not grasp for one second how God was allowing this complicated situation, and I could not fathom how God would shape our life and family. I wanted our life to be our life. I didn't want our life to be Kelci's life. I understood her desire to live in such a beautiful place with a potentially beautiful life with Tyler, but that was not our life. I could see David's desperation as he missed his son. I was utterly stuck. I didn't know what to do. I pleaded and begged God for direction.

Finally, one evening, as David showed me prospective homes and jobs, I blurted out that I could not move. I just couldn't do it—not then, anyway. I was not ready. It was too soon. I already had a heap of change I was trying to sift through. Moving to another state was unthinkable. It was heart-wrenching to tell him these things as he missed his son, but I couldn't keep it in.

We were truly stuck between a rock and a hard place.

We had committed our lives to each other but already felt miles apart. This was not what we were expecting in our first months of marriage. This was outside our plan.

That night, we sat in anguish on the end of our mattress and prayed. We spoke boldly to God and told Him we did not know what to do. We felt like we were in a vise, and the pressure was building. At that moment, we heard God tell us we needed to wait for one year. We both agreed that would be wise. Giving it a timeline made sense to me.

This situation was divisive for me and my family. They did not understand why I would even consider moving away so soon after loss and remarriage. They were relieved to hear we were putting it on hold as they were not ready to let us go.

To make this all happen, we needed to move out of my house into something temporary we could call our own. I wasn't ready to sell my house, but we needed to live somewhere that wasn't tied to either of our pasts.

We immediately began preparing my home for rent. I interviewed property management companies and started decluttering. I had always wondered how long I would live in that house, so it was surreal planning to move. At the same time, we were touring homes for rent in our area.

We realized the rent in the neighborhood where I lived was above our budget, so we began looking at homes in other parts of the city. I was concerned about the boys remaining in the same school, so we knew it could not be too far.

The day after school ended, we packed up my home of almost eleven years and walked out the door. I knew I would be back since we were only renting it out, but it was a brutal loss. I spent time taking pictures of the bare walls and intentionally remembering the life Benji and I lived there. We lived a whole life inside those walls, and as much as it was time to leave, I didn't know how to let go. But with David holding my hand, I kissed the walls goodbye and walked out. The boys took one last look and jumped off the front stoop.

We ended up in a cute, tiny, split-level home near my

parents. We pulled up to unload the first carload of packed boxes. We stepped out of the car, stood on the grass, took a deep breath, and looked at each other with stunned relief. We had a home of our own. Temporary, but it was ours.

The house was slightly run down, but with a good run through the yard and some fresh paint on the front door and living room, it began to feel like ours. I took pride in our little rental, even though it did not belong to us.

We signed a one-year lease and were determined to pray our way through the coming year, hoping God would give us direction on where we should be. We arranged for Harlo to visit, and many times, either David or I would fly to Seattle in the morning, pick up or drop off Harlo with his mom at baggage claim, and fly home the same day. It was brutal on so many levels, but we were thankful God provided a way for us to see him.

Jonah and Isaac would get so excited about Harlo's visits. They always had swords and Nerf guns waiting so they could wage war on us parents. We would play silly games in the dark before bed, and the boys would giggle in delight.

That summer, we took a road trip through Idaho and Oregon to spend time with David's family. I became so fond of his family and thankful for how they truly embraced the boys and me. We celebrated Harlo's fourth birthday, and the boys played with their cousins.

As the trip continued, we headed north to drop Harlo off in Gig Harbor and celebrate his birthday with his mom and friends. This second trip to Washington was met with a little bit more peace. I could see us living in such a beautiful place, but I was still unsure how that would all work out. The obstacles were mountainous, and I knew it would take many God-sized miracles to pull it off.

We arrived home only to greet yet another September and the two-year anniversary. Without truly understanding the toll grief took on me, I pulled David through the triggers and the trauma. He was accepting the excruciating reality he was married to a widow, not only a widow but a woman grieving, loving, and missing another man.

He stayed strong and supported me the best he could, but

it was a wedge in our relationship that was challenging to walk through. David stood silently by as I waded through the trauma of my body, remembering the events that had happened only two years earlier. It always astonished me that I could experience the heavy milestones physically and emotionally. My body remembered in brutal ways, and I needed to come to terms with the fact my body would show signs of trauma for years to come.

I relived the terror of watching Benji take his last breath and woke at precisely 4 a.m. on the morning of the 7th. I was feeling the grief from head to toe. I was recounting the nightmare days of Benji's death at a cellular level and was consumed by sadness. I could barely hold up my head as the days slowly passed: the 7th was his death anniversary, the 8th was Jonah's birthday, and September 15th would have been our fifteenth wedding anniversary.

There was something less celebratory about the second death anniversary. The first year was exciting in a twisted sort of way. I had survived all the significant milestones. I felt like shouting and praising God for getting through something so horrible. But now, I had done it again, and the idea I had countless more years of grief to live was heavier than I could carry. God held me up. He kept His promise to stay close and comfort me.

After the week passed, I began to retake full breaths and left the tight, short gasps behind. I began to see color again, and I was exceedingly grateful to be waking up next to a man who sweetly held my broken heart. This was a gift. A gracious gift from a loving Father who, amid pain, was eager to lavish on me the excellent gift of new love.

David was patient with us and was experiencing trauma in his own way, watching his new family suffer, but this was just another weaving of our lives together. The deep bonding of our lives and our stories grafted into us.

The boys started school that week, and since I didn't want them dealing with another change, I made the twenty-minute drive to Sugarhouse every morning and every day after school so they could stay in the same school. I was willing to spend the extra time in the car to create some normalcy for them. The loss needed to happen in stages. Them being in a familiar place with familiar faces was something I could give them. Having that extra time with them in the car was a blessing. We always arrived early, parked behind the school, and played Mad Libs on my phone. I cherished that time and was thankful they could still laugh and enjoy life.

This was a confirmation we were still in the right place. We were letting go of our way of life slowly and methodically. Losing Benji, although it was expected, felt so abrupt. One day, he was alive and in our home, and the next day, he was gone forever.

I could feel God taking His time as He slowly released us in the rebuilding. He was careful not to shock our systems again. I trusted His timing, even though it was so challenging to have Harlo so far away. It was hard on David's heart, but He trusted Harlo would be okay and that God had us all wrapped up in His arms until we could all be together again.

We continued in therapy. However, my therapist moved out of state, so we began meeting on Skype. The boys transitioned to another therapist who played with them, observed them, and assured me they were doing what was expected. Jonah was the academic one who always wanted to play a board game, and Isaac always chose the black playdough. There was a fascinating psychology behind his color choice. He was still trying to wrap his head around death, and black made the most sense to him.

Jonah began to ask questions about Benji and his sickness one night before bed. It was the first time he vocalized his wonderings and allowed himself to feel the pain outwardly. I stood on the side of the top bunk as he looked up at me with his big, brown, tear-filled eyes. I was powerless to stop the flow and ached to be able to control the pain. I comforted him the best I knew by listening, affirming, and allowing him the space to question.

Isaac was much less aware of the loss at this point. It was abstract and confusing.

I continued to parent them, love them, and create spaces for their grief. It was fragile, but I knew God had them.

Chapter 9
The One Where Everything Changed ... Again

"By faith Abraham, when called to go to a place he would later receive as his inheritance, obeyed and went, even though he did not know where he was going."
Hebrews 11:8

A Hard Journey to the Good

As the idea of a book began to take root, I realized I still desired to finish my English degree, which I had ditched so many years before. I started researching creative writing programs, and after a long process, I was accepted to Southern New Hampshire University to begin finishing my Creative Writing and English degree.

It was daunting and intimidating, but once I began classes, I envisioned myself as a writer and author one day and gained a deep passion for writing and storytelling. The online program catered to my stay-at-home mom life, and I could study and work while the boys were at school. I began watching my new niece, River, once a week, and we had Harlo for about ten days every six weeks or so. David was busy working, and we felt as if we had landed in a soft place. The kids were doing well in school, and we enjoyed living closer to my family. We felt safe. But we knew it was temporary. We felt a shift and change as moving to Washington was heavy in our minds. I was still resistant to the change and was deathly worried for the well-being of my boys.

During the first year of loss, we went to Benji's grave on the seventh of every month. It was a tradition we held to honor him. After the first year, we went when it was on our hearts. I let the boys lead in their desire to spend time there. We only lived a few minutes from the cemetery in our rental home. I knew God needed us to be close for that time. God always knows exactly where we need to be. That is a truth I clung to as we contemplated moving to an entirely new place.

As the holidays approached, the vise became tighter. Harlo's trips were wonderful but taxing on his little body and mind. One day, after Harlo had returned to his mom's, we were sent a text explaining he had digestive and behavioral issues when he went back home to Washington. The traveling back and forth was too much for his little body and mind. This tore us up inside. We felt guilty we weren't closer. We felt anguish over a situation we had no control over. I felt the only solution was to surrender my children and move. This still did not make sense to me as a mom who had lost a husband and was raising boys who had lost their daddy. How could moving away be the best thing for us right now?

Having to pick between children is what nightmares are made of. How could I choose another child's well-being over my own children?

We felt we had two choices. We would either stay in Utah and only see Harlo over the holidays or in the summer. Shuffling him back and forth was clearly not sustainable. Or we could move to Gig Harbor, uprooting our lives and welcoming change that, as a mom, I could only envision would bring emotional damage to my boys. I was torn in every fiber of my being.

What do you do when you need to trust God with the heaviest and most sacred parts of your life? How do you reconcile confusing and nonsensical circumstances with a gracious and loving God?

We read in Genesis about Abraham. He was a man committed to a loving God. He was promised a child at an old age, and although it seemed impossible, He trusted God would deliver, not because He could see how it could happen, but because he trusted the character of God. Abraham trusted God earlier in life when He told him to leave all he had ever known and move to a faraway land, and he chose to trust Him now. And guess what? God came through and kept His promise. At the ripe age of ninety, his wife Sarah gave birth to a son they named Isaac, which means "laughter." (Side note: We named our son Isaac expecting him to make us laugh, and Isaac exceeded our expectations; he makes us belly laugh every day).

In Genesis chapter 22, we read that God had a seemingly unreasonable ask of Abraham. After giving him a son and promising the earth would be blessed through his descendants (Gen. 22:18), God asked Abraham to sacrifice his son Isaac on the altar. At first glance, this seems horrific and so unlike the excellent character of God. But when we take a closer look, we can see the superb nature of God shine, and the story of the faithful and ultimate sacrifice of Jesus come to life.

A Hard Journey to the Good

Abraham had experienced God miraculously and had all the reasons to trust God with this request. He expected God to come through for him and knew God was using the enormous task to prove His trustworthy character further. When they reached the top of the mountain where the altar was, Isaac asked where the lamb for the sacrifice was. Abraham replied, "God himself will provide the lamb" (Gen 22:8). Abraham trusted.

Ultimately, God provided a lamb and let Isaac off the hook. But Abraham was ready to do as God asked, expecting bigger things to happen.

This paints a beautiful picture of our salvation through Jesus Christ on the cross. We are sinners deserving of death, but Jesus is the precious lamb provided to take our place (John 1:29).

I longed to have faith like Abraham, and during these months of contemplating moving, I envisioned "sacrificing" my children in a much more subtle way, of course. I didn't understand the request, but I trusted God because I had seen Him come through before. I trusted God because I knew He was taking care of them. I trusted God because I ultimately believed He sacrificed His son so I didn't have to pay the penalty for my sin. If Jesus could sacrifice His life for me, I could surrender my children and trust God to move, right?

Considering my circumstances, was I willing to put my kids out there, to truly put them in God's hands and trust Him with the outcome?

David and I sat agonizing over the dire circumstances one cold December night. We wrung our hands in confusion and despair. We were six months into our one-year agreement with God but felt the weight of the decision heavy on our shoulders.

This needed to be clarified.

I didn't want to do this.

I wanted it all to go away.

I didn't want to try to explain this to my family.

I wasn't ready for more ridicule.

I couldn't do this.

I was confused, angry, and resentful of my situation,

especially after all I had been through.

Really God? Now this?

We sat and prayed, and in that precious moment, I felt a calm in my spirit. I knew what I was supposed to do. It was the exact opposite of what made sense to me.

I was willing to let everything go, set aside my resentment and uncertainty, trust God, and say yes to moving to Washington.

I held this fragile moment and told Dave we needed to make a statement of faith—not just noddingly agree, but saying it out loud for God and ourselves to hear. We prayed, "Okay, God, we will move."

The clouds lifted off my soul in that divine December moment, with snow flurries blowing outside the window. The burdensome weight I had been lugging around was taken off my shoulders. God stepped into view, and I gave him my boys with all the trust in my frail, grieving body. I ungripped my hands and presented my precious boys to my faithful Father.

I took a deep breath and opened my eyes to the long journey ahead. Without the weight of my resistance holding me back, I knew I had the bravery and courage to take the steps toward Washington. It was blurry, and the road was uncharted, but I trusted God. I trusted He would get us there at the perfect time, and my boys would be more than okay. God made me brave.

Our first Christmas as a new family was festive and beautiful. We celebrated with Benji's family and now had a whole new family through David to spend time with. We felt supported and loved but knew the lingering reveal of our plan to move to Washington was waiting for us in the new year.

As the new year began, we continued to fly Harlo back to us for visits. We flew with our boys to Gig Harbor in March to show them where we'd be moving. We made the best of the super quick trip and hoped God would move in their little hearts and create excitement for a new adventure.

The prospect of moving was beyond daunting. David would need to find a job, and we would need to find a place to live. It seemed impossible. I knew people moved to different states daily, but we needed to figure out where to start.

We began to seek construction jobs and look at homes for rent. We decided to continue renting my house for a time to keep that investment. We slowly started revealing our plan to our families. They could see it was wearing on our little family to keep spending money on flying Harlo back and forth and it was taxing on us emotionally. They could see our desperation to be a complete family, all living in the same place. As we started to tell everyone, we were met with sadness yet equal support. They were devastated at the idea of us living so far away, but they understood.

They could also see that living in Salt Lake was hard for me, and I needed a new start. Everywhere I went, I was faced with a Benji memory. It wasn't always a bad thing, but it was emotionally challenging. They could see a fresh start for our family would be beneficial. I was getting used to the idea of being known as David and Heidi, not widowed Heidi and her new husband, David. I was keen on being in a place that was just ours. Yes, we did know Harlo's mom, but we knew there was a space in Washington to create a life just for us.

After we were married, we continued attending City Church, which David attended when we were dating. I said goodbye to Capital because the memories, though precious, were tainted with images of Benji's funeral. It was hard to walk into the building, and I needed something new. It was just another layer of loss.

City Church was the perfect place to get plugged in and involved. We loved serving together. We volunteered at all sorts of events and made new friends. It was hard to envision leaving that church, but we were fully supported and trusted that God would have the perfect church waiting for us in Gig Harbor.

It was hard for my parents to let us go. When we told them we were moving, they glowed with disappointment, but they knew what was best for our family. Benji's family reacted the same way. They hated that the boys would no longer be around but understood this was needed. I truly began to see that as well. It filled me with peace to let go of my resentment and bitterness at moving and to let God's hand take over as we began preparing to head out of Utah.

In April, we flew up to Washington with my parents to show them the area and look for a home. It was freshly spring, and the flowers were in full bloom. We stayed at a bed and breakfast in the Harbor, and we showed them around downtown. We hired a real estate agent who drove us around looking for prospective rentals. We quickly learned there would be many downsides to renting a home compared to purchasing a home. It would only be temporary in a rental, and the boys would need to move schools at some point if we had to move again. Also, the rental prices were more than a mortgage would be. This threw a wrench in the plan as we added selling my home and getting approved for a mortgage to our list of moving to-dos.

David had an interview while we were there but felt defeated as he realized the job wouldn't work out. We met at the bed and breakfast at the end of the day, and David went straight to our room. He was full of defeat and overcome with the astounding task of finding a job that would pay enough to get us approved for a loan. He was frustrated we were looking at homes but were not even in the place to make an offer. I left him alone and went to the patio to spend time with my parents. We discussed the situation, and they encouraged me it would all work out. I knew what God said. I knew He told us to move, and I trusted it would happen, even if I couldn't see it right then. My mom said, "You will look back at this conversation when you are all settled here in Gig Harbor and remember God's faithfulness." I hoped her words were valid and strived to believe in what I couldn't see.

We returned to Utah empty-handed, though we gained a better understanding of Gig Harbor and the areas we liked.

In a weird twist of Godly circumstances, David's parents, who lived half the year in Palm Desert, CA, had friends whose son owned a construction company in Gig Harbor. They suggested Dave meet him as he may be able to hire him as a carpenter. David reached out to Darren and learned that his daughter, Carlie, babysat Harlo. Darren's wife had her eyelashes done by Kelci. It was a strange coincidence, and we realized how small Gig Harbor was. We were moving to a small town, something we were not used to.

Even though David had a job somewhat waiting for him, the pay was much less than we hoped to earn. David returned to Gig Harbor a few weeks later and had seven interviews in one day. He spent an exhausting day jumping around Tacoma and Gig Harbor as I stayed home in constant prayer he would find something that suited him well and would be able to help us get approved for a home loan. In the meantime, I was busy getting my home ready to sell. It needed a few minor repairs and a good cleaning, and then it was on the market. My dear friend, Josh, was my real estate agent and was able to get it advertised and promoted. It was strange seeing a for sale sign in the front yard. Just another step away from the life I had always known.

When David arrived home from trekking across Washington for interviews, he was hopeful for a few but knew deep down that none of them would be a good fit. He was determined to find the perfect job and extensively tried to manifest what we wanted. However, it left him feeling depleted and overwhelmed. One evening, as we sat in defeat, I simply suggested that maybe since Darren had offered him a job, even though the pay wasn't much, perhaps that was what God wanted. He picked up the phone that evening and accepted the job offer.

We were able to see how God had generously handed David a job, but in our human minds, it wasn't good enough. We wasted several weeks and a lot of mental energy trying to manifest what we thought would be the perfect job, but God had already made it happen. We just overlooked the gift, causing us much grief and stress. We were reminded that God ultimately has our good in mind, even if we can't see it. We read in Proverbs 3:5-6, "Trust in the Lord with all your heart and lean not on your own understanding; in all your ways submit to him, and he will make your paths straight." God knows the way we should go.

Even as you seek the Lord, it is easy to be distracted and get entangled in what we can see with our human eyes. We forget that God has a bigger plan and purpose and can see well beyond anything we can.

Now that we had a job lined up, we needed to apply for a home loan. With my home still for sale, it was challenging as we would need the equity from that home as a down payment for a new home. We went through all the logistics of getting approved and were finally ready to buy a home, with high hopes that my home would sell quickly.

We planned to fly to Seattle for just one night to spend two full days looking at homes. The day before we left, I got an offer on my house. It had only been on the market for one week. God's hand was clearly on this move. We arrived in Gig Harbor and began the hunt for our new home. Our real estate agent drove us around as we looked at numerous houses.

During our time of waiting and contemplating moving, David and I prayed together every single night. When we got married, our pastor told us to pray every night, thanking God specifically for each other. We prayed for our future and God's perfect plan. We lifted moving in prayer and prayed for what we wanted in a new home. We prayed for a home in a safe neighborhood, full of families. We prayed it would be filled with friends for our kids and a great school.

We had these specifics in mind as we hunted but were coming up short. We needed a four-bedroom house, but they were hard to come by. The homes we toured required too much work or were not on a pleasant street. By the end of the first day, we went to bed feeling defeated as we didn't like any of the homes we toured. We lay in bed scrolling real estate apps and saving homes to see the next day.

By the afternoon of the second day, we had narrowed it down to two houses—the ones we hated the least. I liked one more, and David the other. We could not agree, so we decided to go our separate ways to think and pray about it for a while.

David took Harlo to a movie, and I went to get my nails

done. After my appointment, I had time to kill, so I pulled up the real estate app and increased the price limit slightly. A house popped up that I had seen before but was out of the price range. I decided to drive by anyway.

If necessary, we could extend our budget a bit so this could be the house we call home.

As I drove up 40th Avenue, I had the strangest sensation this would be our home. I brushed it off as wishful thinking but couldn't shake it.

I sat in front of the home in the idyllic neighborhood and felt immense excitement and peace. I arranged for our agent to meet us at the house for a tour at 4 p.m. I drove to the movie theater to pick up the boys and anticipated David's reaction as I told him about the home. "Just one more home, I promise." He rolled his eyes in agreement.

As we pulled onto the tree-lined street to the home, the school bus dropped off a gaggle of kids. We slowly drove through the crowd, and I saw groups of moms talking and kids running through the grass and climbing trees. "This is exactly where I want to live," I said, matter of factly. As we got out of the car and waited for the agent to arrive, I was trying to hold back tears. I felt so strongly this was our home, and we had not even walked in yet. And through the bushes popped the neighbor. "Hey, are you gonna be our new neighbors?" he asked excitedly. "We aren't sure," we replied, but we were touched by Greg's enthusiasm to have new neighbors. He told us he had a young son who would be thrilled to have three boys move in next door. We already felt loved and welcomed in this new place.

Our realtor, Jeremy, pulled up, and we walked into the house. I felt like I was floating as I could see this home checked all the boxes. It had enough bedrooms. It had a grand staircase as you walked in the front door, just like the movies. It had a big yard for the kids. It was dated but not anything we couldn't live with for a few years. I saw loads of potential and envisioned our kids running through the halls. David was on a completely different plane as he walked through the home, arms folded, repeating, "Nope, it's too expensive. We can't afford this." I knew it was ours, and God would make a way.

Our agent looked up the details of the home and was convinced it was overpriced. He advised us to make a low offer. We drove to his office, signed a bid of $40,000 below asking, went to the airport, and flew back to Salt Lake to wait.

The next day, we received a counteroffer of only $5,000 off the asking price, so I requested that we meet halfway between our first offer and their counteroffer.

They accepted.

As the text came through, we stood in the kitchen, and I yelled, "They accepted." David grabbed me, lifted and swung me around. God's faithfulness shined through our elated faces. The kids rejoiced, and although they were still not keen on moving, they could sense this was a good thing.
God was making a way where there wasn't a way.

I was so thrilled I almost forgot we still had a long journey ahead.

As we went through the process of selling my home and simultaneously purchasing a home in Washington, stress levels were exceedingly high.

Almost every day, I would get a text or a call from our loan officer or real estate agent explaining some complexity that may prevent us from purchasing the home in Gig Harbor. I would have to boldly bring it back with each situation and remember God's promises, remember that He told us we would move. Even though I could see it all crumbling so many times, leaving us homeless, I trusted God.

He was making a way. God was on the move.

As school ended, we began to say our goodbyes. We finally had a moving date and a moving truck scheduled. The reality of leaving all we had ever known was closing in on us.

I was leaving Utah. I was leaving Benji there in his grave. I was battling feelings of guilt. I was fighting feelings of sorrow. As I was being torn away but given a new life, I was living in a tension of grief and joy. Loss and hope. Mourning and laughter.

Joshua 1:9 was posted on my bathroom mirror during this tumultuous time of transition, and I read the words over and over to remind myself that God would be with me in Washington.

Have I not commanded you? Be strong and courageous. Do not be afraid; do not be discouraged, for the Lord your God will be with you wherever you go.

I was not alone as I walked out the unbearable goodbyes that would lead to a new life. I would not be alone when I arrived in my new home, and I would not be alone as I continued to walk out a life without Benji.

A few weeks later, I drove up to my Sugarhouse home and made final adjustments before handing over the keys. This time, the goodbye would be permanent. I could barely walk out the door. I was walking out of that house with ten years of Benji memories. How could it just be over? How could I just leave it? I again fought feelings of guilt and anguish over moving forward in my life. Although that is precisely what he would want for us—a new life and adventure—I still felt like I was abandoning him. I couldn't shake the feeling he was still in the walls. He was still in the backyard brewing beer. He was still wrestling with the boys in the living room. He was still lying in our bedroom, taking in his last days on earth.

I pushed through the excruciating pain and walked out the back door one last time. I drove to the real estate office, signed the closing papers, handed over Benji's death certificate and our house keys, and left.

The home was gone. That life was over.

But what awaited me was a rental house full of packed boxes, our life in cardboard, ready to be driven to our new life. I was able to take a deep breath of relief. I had said goodbye to my home with Benji, something I had been dreading. Another layer of loss was removed.

God allowed a loss so big it almost swallowed me whole. But the loss was not just Benji. As I continued to live, there were a million tiny losses I had to experience. I continued to walk through them as some rushed over me with sadness, and some I could walk firmly through, having hope on the other side.

Jonah and Isaac had their last day of school at the beginning of June. This was not a "see you after summer" goodbye. It was goodbye, forever. As we walked out of the school, I quickly stopped in the office to say goodbye and thank the excellent staff who had helped me navigate those first few agonizing weeks and months after the loss. They supported me as a mom and helped the boys adjust to life after Daddy. I could not leave without acknowledging their place in my healing.

We walked out the doors into the fresh summer air, a new adventure on the horizon. I held that moment with the boys and had them recognize that juncture in our new life. This was the last time they would ever step into that school—another loss.

Our house began to look like a miniature city with boxes stacked high. My mom and Vanessa were there to help me articulate packing for a long trip in a moving truck. We had Harlo one last time just before we moved, and we spent a weekend camping with my family, Josh, and his family. We took in the memories as we knew it would be a long time before we were all together again. David and I captured the moment by photographing the breathtaking, colorful Utah sunset. The goodbyes and losses were now piling on top of each other.

One evening, we took a break from packing, and I took the two boys to Smashburger, our favorite place. We ordered and sat down. I was buried in my phone as the logistics of selling a home and buying a home in another state were all-consuming. My boys were joyous and not seated in silence. They were loud and rambunctious, but it wasn't bothering me. A lady with a cane walked up to me and said gently, "Your boys are so well-behaved." In an odd way, I said, "Thank you." and she harshly replied "I was being sarcastic! Your boys are out of control, and you're buried in your phone." I was dumbfounded at her rude comment and was shocked silent. I grabbed our food and the boys, and we left. I was bubbling up inside. I wanted to give that lady a piece of my mind, but of course, I only found the right words after I had left. I posted about the situation on FB and vented my feelings. This lady had no right to judge my mothering. She had no idea they had lost their daddy, and we were all preparing to leave the only home we had ever known. I should never be buried in my phone in the presence of my kids, but I wasn't scrolling needlessly. I was handling heavy-duty logistics that at the moment needed to be dealt with. Death and moving are listed as the most stressful events in a human life, and she had no idea. She made a judgment call on my mothering. In my eyes, the fact that my boys were happy and filled with joy in spite of their life-altering circumstances was reason enough for me to let them be themselves in the restaurant. I am sure I looked like an air-head mom, and I certainly felt like one, but I couldn't let the guilt and offense take over. Instead, I reminded people not to judge other people.

  The boys and I had continued to meet at the Sharing Place, which created deep friendships and connections with others who had experienced profound loss. The support we gained there was phenomenal, and I don't see how I could have survived without other widows and counselors to lean on.

  We said goodbye to our friends at the Sharing Place. When we left, they gave me a small fabric bag with a string to cinch up the top. When I reached inside, I could feel a rock that was rough and coarse, and I could also feel a smooth, sleek rock. I was told that these rocks represented the boys and me when we first walked into that musty room on that dark, cold November night, and the other rock represented us now. Some of our edges had been smoothed, and we had gained healing and fortitude to be able to move into the next chapter of our lives. I keep this bag in my jewelry drawer, and every once in a while, I will reach in the bag to remember the place we were so long ago and the place we are now.

  We had a going away party at my parents' house and

invited anyone we could think of. It was a gorgeous summer night, surrounded by everyone who loved us. We saw family, old high school friends, Benji's work friends, and church friends. Friends from all walks of life. I was reminded of Benji's funeral when I was surrounded by all the people Benji and I had ever known. This was the same but different. We were gathering because of the loss again, but this time, it was a good loss. A loss that brought hope. A loss that we could see past. This time, it was a loss that we welcomed.

Chapter 10
The One With a New Life

"How lucky I am to have something that makes saying goodbye so hard."
Winnie the Pooh[10]

A Hard Journey to the Good

A Hard Journey to the Good

When Benji and I were both thirty, we thought trying something new would be so fun. We made our way up the mountain to place a snowboard on our feet and attempt to slide down the side of the hill. What were we thinking?

Apparently, you can teach an old dog new tricks, but not without excruciating pain and embarrassment.

We took lessons and were placed in a class of teenagers and younger people who caught on much quicker than we did. That first winter, we spent more time falling than gliding. However, we stuck with it, and amidst the hard crashes, we were starting to see the beauty and rush of descending a snow-packed mountain, wind in our faces, and adrenaline pumping. We were alive. We were living this life together.

We continued snowboarding together until he became sick, and then it was just me going alone with our friends. During those snowboarding days, I missed him sitting next to me on the ski lift as we discussed technicalities and what we had learned on our last, brutal run.

I lost him in this long before he left.

As David, the boys, and I prepared to leave Utah, I was consumed with memories as I took in the vast mountain range that towered over the city. These mountains were my home. My childhood was spent camping in the warm summer air in those mountains. I had spent a million hours hiking, mountain biking, snowboarding, and picnicking in those mountains. They greeted me every moment of my life as the sun peeked over the white snowcaps. Fall colors painted them in oranges and reds, and the winters clothed them in brilliant white. These mountains housed Benji and me as we careened down the hills with our lives on the line, and these mountains witnessed us as I took Benji for his last mountain drive up Millcreek Canyon just days before he died. I photographed him sitting on a large rock at the base of one of our favorite hikes. For years after, I took a photo of my boys sitting on the same stone—a place of remembrance.

These mountains cradled David and me as we said "I do" amidst the frozen winter wonderland. These mountains were another immense loss. I knew Washington had mountains, but not these mountains.

The sizable moving truck arrived at our home, and several strong men started organizing and placing boxes in the truck. We sat on the front lawn and watched our entire lives, now all mixed together, be packed and sent to a new place—our promised land.

When the Israelites arrived at the Jordan River and could see the promised land in the distance, some chose to stay behind. They were comfortable in the desert. They didn't want to bring about unnecessary change, even though they knew God had promised them this land. They chose to rebel against God because they feared what would be on the other side: "The people are stronger and taller than we are; the cities are large, with walls up to the sky" (Deuteronomy 1:28).

It is so much easier to stay where it is comfortable because we are afraid of the unknown and unable to see past the challenges we will likely face on the other side. Moses assured them they would be taken care of as he told his people, "'Do not be terrified; do not be afraid of them. The Lord your God, who is going before you, will fight for you, as he did for you in Egypt, before your very eyes, and in the wilderness. There you saw how the Lord your God carried you, as a father carries his son, all the way you went until you reached this place.' In spite of this, you did not trust in the Lord your God, who went ahead of you on your journey, in fire by night, and in the cloud by day, to search out places for you to camp and to show you the way you should go" (Deuteronomy 1:29-33).

These are the promises I clung to as each box placed in the moving truck solidified our decision to move. There was no going back now.

During our time in that rental home, our cat had kittens. It was a precious experience for our boys to have seven kittens in the house. We gave away six of them and kept one. His name was Venus. On the day of the move, we tried desperately to gather the cats. We were successful in snagging Zazzles, the mom, but Venus refused. He did not want to come with us. As we got in the car to leave Utah, Jonah cried. He loved that cat and didn't understand why the cat didn't want to come. I assured him the cat was happy where he was, living in all the neighborhood backyards. The cat was happy even though we were not. I didn't understand why Jonah faced another loss as we drove away from home, but I still trusted God there was purpose in that pain.

Almost six months from the day Dave and I had boldly prayed our "yes" to God, we were on the road. Home sold. Home purchased. Boxes packed and gas tanks full. Dogs nestled in the front seat with me, the fish sat safely in the console next to our jar of colored, layered sand from our wedding, and Jonah was in the back seat, scared and confused by the move but brave and excited. Dave and Isaac were in his truck with Zazzles, and the back filled to the brim with all the odds and ends that didn't fit in the moving truck.

The moving truck was scheduled to land at our new home on July 1st, so we had two days to trek from Salt Lake to Gig Harbor.

Before we got on the highway, we made one last stop at my parents' house. This was what I had dreaded the most: saying goodbye to my family. A few days earlier, I said goodbye to my sister, Chelsea, Waid, and River. Leaving baby River ripped my heart out more than any other goodbye. I was devastated to no longer be around for her growing up. However, I was extremely thankful for the opportunity to watch her once a week over that last year. It created such a strong bond between us that is still strong today. I was devastated to leave my only sister. We had bonded so much since she had her daughter, and I hated that we wouldn't be doing mom things together.

My baby brother, Nick, lived in Denver, and we had already said our sad goodbyes when he moved there a year earlier. The boys were devastated. He had been the man in their life. Thankfully, at that point, David had already come into the picture to ease the sting.

All of the relationships that had healed over that last

year were astounding. God had a solid plan in having us wait to move. He needed to do some mighty healing work in the hearts of everyone who loved Benji the most. We spent that year healing those relationships. Benji's friends slowly accepted David into our lives. Benji's family came to know David and how good he was for the boys and me. All the resentment and anger melted away that year. We were able to leave with love and support. If we had moved right away, none of that healing would have occurred. We would have suffered the consequences if we had ignored God's perfect plan. David would never have had a space to come into those sacred places. Hearts would have stayed hard. Healing would have been stunted.

God's miraculous hand had held us all right where we needed to be, and now we were being released into the new life waiting for us in the Pacific Northwest. We were able to leave with peace.

I hugged my parents and began to walk to the car. I turned back and ran into their arms again. Tears flowing. Hearts pounding. I was bereaved to leave my parents and my people. I felt sorry for them as they said goodbye to their oldest daughter, who they had seen experience deep heartache and tragedy. They had lost their son-in-law almost three years earlier, and this new loss came much too soon. I was thankful for their understanding at that moment. They didn't understand at first, but God lifted the weight off of them as well. They had peace in their hearts about us moving. They were willing to sacrifice their daughter and her family for them all to experience new life, more healing levels, and God's abundant goodness. They could see past the rough waters of the Jordan River into our promised land.

I let go of my parents, walked to my car, and drove away. The salty tears felt excruciating as they fell down the worn grooves in my skin. I had always lived near my parents and no longer did.

We got on the highway and drove north on I-15, passing the city, and the memories popped up from all walks of my life. I took in all thirty-six years of life and said goodbye to Salt Lake as we drove around the point of the mountain, the city disappearing from view and onto new and bigger things.

David's mom and dad lived in Boise, almost halfway between Salt Lake and Gig Harbor. It was a perfect place to land for a rest. As we spent time with his family that evening, I received a call from the moving company explaining they would deliver our things that next morning. One problem. We would not be there yet.

Our original move-in date was June 30th, but we had changed it to July 1st. I had done all the necessary paperwork to change the moving date in writing, but unfortunately, that did not get into the right hands. The moving truck would be there on the wrong date. I was furious. They said it was because of staffing; we would now need to wait two to three weeks for our things to arrive. They emptied our entire moving truck into an unknown warehouse in Seattle. I would not take that for an answer. We only had some of our clothes and odds and ends. We didn't know anyone we could stay with. We needed our things. We pleaded our case and waited to hear back. As we had dinner with family that night, the idea that our items were sitting in a warehouse somewhere unknown, perhaps mixed up with someone else's things, perhaps in an unsecured area, possibly lost, was very unsettling for me.

It was another roadblock in our move, and the stress was mounting. The promised land was within our reach, but the roadblocks made the waters of the Jordan River so rough. Still, we trusted God would make a way.

The following day, we left Boise's dry air and headed to Puget Sound. We trusted our stuff would eventually make it and continued on the road to our new life.

As we drove across the dusty Idaho and Oregon deserts, I thought about our new life on the horizon: new friends, new church, new people, new experiences. The canvas of our new life was clean, white, and fresh. I had said a scary yes to God and trusted Him with the rest. I gave God that paintbrush and trusted He would create something beautiful.

We passed over the border between Oregon and

Washington, and Isaac commented how he had anticipated a dense forest to greet us over the border, but we were still in the desert. "This doesn't look very planty," he commented as we drove over the bridge. My mom's heart giggled as they were anticipating their new life.

As we drove the eight hours towards Seattle, we ended up on 1-5 in traffic. Welcome to the Seattle area. Gridlock.

We coordinated to meet our real estate agent at the title office as we had one more paper to sign before we could grab our keys. Just one more hurdle. One more wave to overcome on the Jordan. We drove over the stunning Tacoma Narrows bridge, pulled into Gig Harbor, and exited the car. The humid summer air greeted us. I couldn't believe we now lived there.

We signed the papers and were handed the keys. The sensation I had been waiting for.

We drove to Harlo's daycare and picked him up before heading to our new home.

I captured the moment as we all walked into our new home, a home the boys had only seen pictures of. We told them to run upstairs and choose their rooms. They did just that, and with giddy laughter, I could hear them giggling and screaming, "I want this one! I want this one!"

Rooms were picked. Deep breaths were taken, and David and I stood in the empty spaces of our new home, bursting with hope and new life. We took a photo of the boys on the front porch. In this surreal moment, I hoped Benji was watching. We took the kids for burgers in our new city and came back to our home with an invitation from our neighbors to come over to meet them. I walked into their backyard and met the people who lived next door, Greg and Sara. These were the people we would do life with, our first friends, and with whom we still, seven years later, share life, trading garden tomatoes and the occasional egg or toilet paper roll.

We chatted that night, and I shared our story. Our conversation was sweet, and we immediately felt loved and anticipated as they told us how excited they had been for us to move in. The boys were already playing with their new friends in the warm summer night air, and we could feel God's hand. I wasn't scared anymore. I had jumped, waddled, and crawled over many hurdles to get to that point. I vowed never to forget God's faithfulness in this experience. I will forever remember this when I come across other obstacles in my life.

We had done it. We trusted God with massive hills of roadblocks and discouragement, and He made a way. It was impossible in our eyes, but God does His best with the impossible.

We walked back home and set up our air mattresses in our bedrooms. David's brother Eric, his wife, Andrea, and their kids Ezra and Ella arrived that night from Oregon. They had agreed to help us move in, and we were so excited to have family close.

The following day, the much-anticipated moving truck arrived. They had moved things around to ensure we had everything on time. We spent the next few days unloading, marking off our giant list of items to ensure we had everything. We did. Everything had arrived.

We celebrated our first holiday in Gig Harbor—the Fourth of July. I was reminded of the fourth two years earlier. As I watched the fireworks explode off the great Mississippi River, I remembered how I was so unsure of my future with David and what my new life would look like.

New life was abounding this Independence Day.

Kelci had access to a private beach park, and we celebrated our country's independence with new friends and an astonishing fireworks display. We imagined it was Washington welcoming us to our new home.

We spent that summer exploring the nearby beaches, parks, and lakes. I took the boys to Seattle via ferry one day and explored Pike Place and Seattle Center. We stood below the Space Needle, taking in the splendor.

I had traveled to Seattle many times and envisioned living there, but it was unreal to me that it was actually happening.

We enjoyed getting to know our new neighbors, and the boys had a gaggle of kids to play with on the streets. It was everything I had hoped for, prayed for, and more.

On July 19th, David and I sat in our bathroom, staring at a little white stick. David sat on the bathtub's edge, and I stood before him as we counted the three minutes until we could look at the results. The timer went off, David peaked at the test, looked up at me with his big brown eyes. "You're totally pregnant!" David wrapped me in his arms as we took in the shock together. We were going to have a baby.

When we first started dating and getting serious, we talked about adding another child to our family, but we weren't sure we wanted to have four children. Over time, as our love grew and we created a new little family, I could not imagine a life without sharing the breathtaking experience of pregnancy and a new baby with David. I desperately wanted to share all the joys and hardships with him. I loved him so much and wanted us to have our own baby. We had his and mine, but we wanted ours. We agreed to wait until after the move. And what do you know? I got pregnant on the first night we moved into our house.

There was no going back now. Our life was on the fast track, and we were just trying to keep up.

I wanted to wait until I saw my family again before I told them, so I would have to wait a crazy long six weeks before we all met in San Francisco for my cousin's wedding.

The weeks leading up to the trip were hot, and I felt terrible. I was convinced that something had died in the pantry as the smell was horrid, but David assured me that all was well. It was just my hormones playing tricks on me.

A few weeks later, we traveled to San Francisco, and I was able to tell my family I was expecting. They were overjoyed at the prospect of a new grandchild and cousin. We all hoped and dreamed that it would be a girl.

As fall approached again, so did my familiar grief symptoms. They were compounded by the boys starting a new school and life-changing so rapidly.

On the first day of school, I walked Jonah to his fourth-grade class and Isaac to his third-grade class. I left them at their desks and kissed them goodbye. I was astounded at their bravery, but my mama's heart broke. I knew being the new kid in school was not easy, and they were far from everything they had ever known. I walked to the car in tears as David assured me they would be okay.

I spent that hard week reliving again the tragic moments that led to Benji's death and all the anxiety the fall air brings. I was living in a tight tension of grief with a baby growing inside my belly. A sign of new life. A new heart and a new precious person who was only alive because Benji died.

Those were hard feelings to trek through. They required a lot of contemplation and time with the Lord. I often felt as though I needed to figure out my feelings and the strange dynamics of my life, but I knew I might never understand, and I just needed to live in thankfulness one day at a time. It was okay to be baffled by my circumstances.

That fall and winter, we settled into our new home and routine. We enjoyed getting to know the area and loved getting to know our neighbors. I continued to work on my online degree and was starting to get used to the rain amid our luscious, green surroundings.

We joined a Foursquare church and felt like we had landed in a solid, safe, and loving place. We were developing strong and long-lasting friendships.

That following spring, I was given my most precious gift from loss. On April 2nd, Emmy Lynn came into our world. Her name means complete. My pregnancy was uneventful, but after a long, excruciating labor almost ending in a C-Section, I could hold the girl I had always dreamed of, the girl Benji always wanted me to have.

I remember sitting on the front porch with Benji in his last days. I remember him telling me he wanted me to move on and marry someone with a little girl. I did him one better; I had a girl of my own—tangible goodness God had promised.

Our three boys were elated. Everyone we knew was ecstatic to witness a precious little girl added to our tribe of boys. We brought her home and jumped into infant life. I was eight years older than when I had Isaac, and it was apparent. I was more tired and could sense my age as I nursed and spent long nights with Emmy. But God gave me the strength and endurance to push through those hard days and weeks of new baby life.

I was beyond thankful I was given this perfect gift of my daughter. I had gotten to a place where the constant change was ending. The past three and a half years since Benji took his last breath left me swirling. I was thankful for our new life. But now, the natural healing was longing to take place. I still had bitter, complex roots to pull out. I still had many triggers to process and countless hours of therapy to pour out my heart.

God met me in all of it. God proved His faithfulness. I had a far-reaching list of experiences that could point to his endless goodness, even in tragedy.

When Emmy was a few weeks old, I held her sweet, sleeping body as I stared at the misty rain melting onto the fresh spring flowers. I took in God's goodness. I vowed to share my story and all God had done. At that moment, I told God I would dedicate my life to illuminating His presence as I pointed to the goodness of God. I knew there was more healing needed. I knew more pain would come. But I also trusted God would bring more good out of my circumstances than I could ever imagine, just like He had always done.

Epilogue

"God whispers to us in our pleasures, speaks to us in our conscience, but shouts in our pains. It is his megaphone to rouse a deaf world."
C.S. Lewis[11]

A Hard Journey to the Good

A Hard Journey to the Good

I have spent the last decade trying to reconcile pain with a good God. How does this occur? How do humans overcome the gnawing questions that protrude from our finite minds? How can a good God allow bad things to happen?

Let's look at some Biblical truths that can help us navigate our questions.

The Good News of the Bible is we have hope beyond anything we see in this world. Death does not have the final say. Just because Benji left his earthly body does not mean death had the last word. He is living in our promised paradise, free of pain and sin.

We read in 1 Thessalonians 4:13, "Brothers and sisters, we do not want you to be uniformed about those who sleep in death, so that you do not grieve like the rest of mankind, who have no hope." With Jesus, we can have the ability to grieve with hope. We have the hope of heaven. We have an eternal perspective that allows us to look at our world through the eyes of Jesus, through the eyes of a loving and good God.

Let's dig in deeper and take it back to the beginning. In the Garden of Eden, God gave Adam and Eve a choice. He had gifted them with perfection, but God wanted to be loved because his people chose to love Him, not because they didn't have a choice.

Genesis 2:15 reads, "The LORD God took the man and put him in the Garden of Eden to work it and take care of it. And the Lord God commanded the man, 'You are free to eat from any tree in the Garden; but you must not eat from the tree of the knowledge of good and evil, for when you eat from it, you will certainly die.'"

They were living in perfection. In the form of a serpent, Satan convinced Eve God was holding out on them, and if they ate the fruit, they would be like God, knowing good from evil (Genesis 3:4). Eve ate the fruit, and, at that moment, sin entered the world, and they immediately knew they were naked. They were kicked out of the garden and told they would live in a world of sin and pain; they would experience the realities of the fallen world.

The narrative of the Bible is the beautiful story of God's redemption plan to save humanity. He came down as a human, Jesus, to rescue us from the nasty world we had landed in. He sacrificed himself on the cross to redeem us from our sins and free us from the power of death.

Because of Jesus, we do not have to live hopelessly in a seemingly hopeless world. We can trust God amid our deepest pains and heartaches.

It is easy to form our own ideas and opinions about how we think things should go. We pray for what we want; sometimes, God's answer is the opposite of what we prayed for. I prayed for my husband to be healed—no, I begged God to heal him.

God didn't heal Benji on earth.

God healed him in heaven. He answered my prayer, just not how I wanted.

I was left to navigate that desperate loss and work hard to reconcile a good God with profound loss. I still don't understand why Benji did not get to live an entire life on earth, but I trust a good God who knows way more than I do.

He knows all the reasons, and He promises to work all things together for good for those who love God (Romans 8:28).

Our view of life is so minimal. We can't see past our own experiences into the vast universe of God, but we can trust the God who sees and knows all. When we can rest in these truths and believe in these promises, it does help us reconcile our pain. When we can surrender all of our why questions, we can sit in the presence of the almighty and know that His mighty hand is at work in our lives when all we see is chaos.

We can rest in Jesus and watch and see how he brings the good.

When Benji first died, I would have recurring dreams of him. In the beginning, I usually dreamt normally of him. Then, I dreamed he had just returned from one of his long trips. Then I got remarried. For years, I dreamed he had returned and wanted everything to return as it was. I knew I needed to tell him I was remarried, but I never could before waking up. Eventually, I could tell him I was remarried, but he was furious I had moved on, so guilt set in . . . then, I dreamed he was happy for me. Then I dreamed I was at his funeral and David was with me. The last dream I had I was sitting at his grave with David's arms around me. Finally closure. That all took nine years. It took nine years to undo in my subconscious, to accept the reality he was gone.

I have lived in the stinging tension between loss and new life in this decade of grief. I have grieved over a myriad of anniversaries, milestones, birthdays, and triggers. I have spent hours upon hours in therapy spewing out all of the complex emotions and intricacies of blended family life mixed with grief.

In one session several years ago, during one of my grief meltdowns, my therapist walked me through a process called Lifespan Integration. I wrote out my entire grief timeline, and she read it back to me, as I was lying on a couch. She told me to go back to a place in my grief, to a place where I was the most vulnerable. I remembered the girl standing in line at the hotel in Disneyland just a few days after Benji died. I remembered a confused and rattled girl struggling to breathe and crawling out of her skin.

In the session, I was able to go back and talk to that girl. I had the opportunity to walk up to her and tell her everything would be okay. By connecting that memory with my current life, I reached a miraculous level of healing. By integrating that time and space with what is going on in my current life, I was able to lessen the grip of grief. I was able to bring healing to that fragile and traumatizing part of my life.

After a decade of loss, I have scrolls full of how God has proven himself faithful. He was devoted to His promise never to leave or forsake me (Deuteronomy 31:6). In those early days, He promised peace (Philippians 4:6-7) and that all of my loss and grief would work together for good (Romans 8:28).

Since moving to Washington, we have lived in the same house, and the kids have saturated themselves in our small community here in the South Sound. We still own the dark gray Pilot I purchased on my own so many Decembers ago. We have put thousands upon thousands of miles on that SUV, taking us from one adventure to the next. I sensed a need for a bigger car way back then, and I can see now it was God nudging me to purchase a car that would one day be needed for a family of six, something I could never have conjured up during that cold, winter day sitting in the Honda dealership. This just proves to be another way God was guiding us to new life. I listened, and I followed, even though I could barely see past the fog on that first winter as a widow.

In our new home, we have been blessed with numerous families, kids, and dear friends who have walked on this journey with us. As people get to know us, we eventually tell them we are a blended family. That statement inevitably leads to more questions. My least favorite is, "Do your boys still have a relationship with their dad?" My response flows from my mouth in familiar tones as I watch the grimace of my new friend as the words "He died of cancer" come out of my mouth. Immediately, there is a deepness in the relationship as they share their condolences, struggling with what to say next. Sometimes, they can relate. Sometimes, it's like I speak a foreign language, and they don't even know what to do with me. I have learned to nod, accept their condolences, and tell them it is okay. For a while, it sounded like a lie because it is never okay Benji died, and I had to live through horrific trauma, climb out of a pit of death, struggle to move forward, and ultimately land me standing there talking to them. I have learned just to say "thank you." Simple. And then, if I sense the need, I change the subject.

I have spent precious moments with my boys as they continue to grieve at each stage of maturity. I've watched them open the letters Benji wrote to them in his last days. They have them tucked away in their "daddy box" printed, typed-out letters labeled for each of them. Their thirteenth birthdays were celebrated but shadowed by Benji's words from beyond. They still have letters to anticipate when they turn eighteen and when they get married.

As they have grown, I have had to prayerfully watch my words as I subtly remind them of milestones or anniversaries. Jonah was just a little bit older than Isaac when Benji passed and has more memories of him and the dramatic events surrounding his death. Jonah remembers his sweet goodbye in the hospital and remembers significant parts of the loss, gifting him with closure. My dear Isaac lives in regret because he declined to say goodbye to Benji on his last day, stealing him of the closure he so desperately wants. I could never have forced a five-year-old to visit his dying father, but we both wish that would have ended differently for him. We have spent dark evenings on the couch, hashing over the details as I remind him he does not need to live in regret. He can't allow the weight of that decision to take a toll on him. He can let the Lord inside those broken parts of his heart and bring healing.

After Isaac was born, Benji and I debated whether to have more children. By the time Isaac was five, Benji was terribly sick. We knew then we felt complete as a family of four. I never thought I would one day have more children. But after my loss, God blessed me with two more littles.

With such a significant age gap, I am noticing how I am getting a second chance at parenting small kiddos. All of the things I miss about the boys being little, I get to do with Harlo and Emmy. I kept most of the boys' books and adore spending nights with Emmy reading her Jonah and Isaac's favorite books, worn and torn. I get to relive their childhood through my daughter. God knew I wasn't ready to be an empty nester in my mid-forties; He knew my mama's heart and gave me more opportunities to have the sweet moments with a precious daughter snuggled up next to me.

When Benji died, I bombarded the boys with weekly therapy as I hoped they would be so well counseled they would not have to take any baggage into their older years. This is something that I tried to control, but over the years, I have learned they each grieve differently. They each hold different memories and hurts in their hearts, and they, perhaps, won't be able to come to terms with the loss until they are fully mature. I pray they will hold Jesus close in the challenging moments of healing and remember the truths I have poured into their hurting hearts over all these years.

David and I have grown and blossomed in our marriage. I have learned how to live in a marriage while grieving another man. David has a way of intently listening as I speak of my dark grief days, and he gives me sweet, strong hugs when he knows it is a hard anniversary day. He is sensitive to my emotions and has learned as much as he can about loss without experiencing it personally. He has become an expert at handling and comforting his grieving wife. He has never been offended or jealous. He has listened to the Lord intently as he has learned when to listen, stay quiet, and speak words of encouragement.

However, grieving in a new marriage has not been easy. Grief has tried to wedge its way into our marriage and tear it apart. Unfortunately, the trauma I experienced has leaked into our new life and caused triggers and trauma to infiltrate our marriage. David often struggles when anniversaries roll around, and we all feel the weight of the September days that tend to creep in every year. Thankfully, we have learned how to grow past these hurts and experiences and allow them to strengthen us and build resilience in our marriage. David wasn't present in my old life, but God has placed him in the new parts of my story, and he is saturated in my journey of healing.

I have witnessed the beautiful bonding between David, Jonah, and Isaac. David has loved them like his own sons. He has been their father much longer than Benji was. Benji parented babies, toddlers, and preschoolers, and David has taken on older kids into their teenage years. David has taught them everything boys need to know about being strong, God-loving men. He has taken his commitment to them seriously, and one year after we got married, he officially adopted them. David remembers the words of Benji from their Bible study together all those years earlier and takes Benji's desire to parent his boys to heart. He is hands-on. He includes them in all of his projects, including carpentry, car repairs, and building.

I have learned to be a bonus mom and graciously parent with another woman. Kelci and I have become best friends over our years of parenting together. She and her husband, Tyler, and their two daughters have formed their own relationships with God, creating a more beautiful and loving blended family than any of us could have imagined. Emmy has gained sisters in this unique family dynamic, and we see God's hand on our family as all the girls cherish their unique sisterly relationship.

My bond with Harlo has grown strong over these years. I strive to love him like my own son. I parent, teach, discipline, and cherish him. His bond with Jonah and Isaac has stretched and morphed over the years. As the older boys have matured into teenagers, their relationship has changed from those early days of sharing bunk beds in our small home in Utah, but I trust in years to come, as they grow older together, God will continue to bring bonding moments. Harlo and Emmy are extra close, and it warms my heart our children love each other so much.

There, unfortunately, is a nasty reality behind all perfectly curated blended families. I don't want to sugarcoat the ugliness that step-parenting can bring. When a baby is born, they are chemically bonded to their parents. This gives the biological parents an instinct and closeness that allows them to love their child in the most intimate way possible.

Step-parents do not naturally have this bond; it is something they have to create. I have seen this on both sides of our family, as it has taken a great deal of intentionality to love Harlo like I do my other children. It doesn't come as naturally some days, and I have to battle with myself to keep calm or not be too hard on him. I see the same with David. He tends to be harder on my boys than on Harlo, and I know that stems from the fact that he is not their biological father. Step-parenting is hard work, and some days, it can be entirely overwhelming. We have had moments of disagreement in our family, and the line starts to be drawn between my boys and me and David and Harlo. The thing that has kept those divisions at bay is our awareness of the growing division and how ugly it feels under our skin. We sink away from those chasms of discord and seek reconciliation and forgiveness. It is challenging and yucky, but we know God wants our family to be united in Him.

David and I have learned how to navigate complex family dynamics that don't make sense. The complexities of our family would crush us if we didn't have Jesus to run to. We have the odd dynamics of one child only with us every other week, we have grieving and growing teenage boys, and we have a little girl who is part of all of us but constantly trying to figure out the crazy dynamics of our home life. She has gained a sweet, empathetic spirit as I tell her about Benji and the loss the boys and I experienced. She has proven to be the most precious gift out of my loss.

Our family has shared countless beautiful conversations about Benji and how to fit his loss into our complex life. We talk about Benji, celebrate his birthday, sit in stillness when his favorite songs come on the radio, and cheer on his beloved Utah Jazz for him.

Not long after we moved to Washington and I was

pregnant with Emmy, we said goodbye to our little pugs, Yoda and Vader. They passed away quietly, one month apart from each other, as I wept next to them. It was just another brutal layer of loss. Those pugs meant the world to Benji. They are now buried in our backyard, nestled among tall pines, signified with stones in remembrance of a life once lived.

In 2022, we welcomed a new puppy into our home. To stay consistent with the Star Wars way of life, we named him Obi-Wan Kenobi. He is a large Aussie doodle and has become a beautiful part of our family.

We traveled back to Utah many times since we left on that hot July day. Each time I return, I am bombarded with memories or triggers I must work through. Some trips feel sweet and kind, while other times, I only sit in the unfairness that the place holds so many hard memories. I have learned to walk through each experience and take each emotion as it comes. I have learned grief is my best friend, my closest companion, and the one thing that keeps Benji close. I have learned living a life full of joy and sorrow is possible at the same time. I don't need to pick between the two. They can both live harmoniously inside my heart.

Homesickness has become a feeling I have to battle time and time again. I often feel left out of birthdays, holidays, and special events with my family in Utah. In 2019, my sister Chelsea and her husband Waid welcomed their second child, a boisterous and inquisitive little guy named Quinn. It breaks my heart to miss out on his growing years, but through Facetime and frequent trips, I have a strong bond with River and Quinn that makes our reunions even more special. River and Emmy claim their best friend status as they play dolls over Facetime and text each other with long rows of ridiculous emojis.

On a recent trip, as I sat on the couch dreading the goodbyes, tears streamed down my face as I cried out to my mom about how unfair it was I must live somewhere else. She assured me God's place for us in Washington is exactly where we need to be. She understood we needed a fresh start so many years earlier and a new home not riddled with memories of loss. We have built a beautiful, full life in our new city, surrounded by deep friendships and support only God could have curated. She comforted my heart and assured me God's plan is bigger and better than what I could conjure up.

Since moving to Washington, my boys have gained a love for wrestling. It seems fitting as that was their favorite activity with their daddy. If you can call loud grunts, rolling around on the rug, and jumping from the couch wrestling.

Both have excelled in their club wrestling, middle school and now into their high school years. They have earned their place in regional and state championships. We have spent many hours on the sidelines cheering on these boys as they are face down on the mats, reaching for their last bits of strength to gain a pin and, ultimately, a victory. David nearly loses his voice as he shouts for them to "dig deep!"

In these sorts of moments, I pull my ball cap over my tear-filled eyes so no one can see the agony leaking from my soul. I am shot back in time to the excruciating moments of loss that seemed to come in waves, like childbearing pains. In the beginning, they were close together, over and over every day. As the years have gone by, the waves come with triggers, and they ache hard. The knot in my stomach tightens as I grin and bear through the physical pain of missing Benji, wishing he could see the boys. I feel utterly alone as no one knows what is pulling me out of my body into a vortex of grief. I swirl, breathe fast, and spin until it starts to slow down, and I land safely back in the bleachers. I take a deep breath, pull up my ball cap, and continue cheering.

This is grief. These rippling moments of despair have overcome me more times than I can count over the last decade, in seemingly small moments and significant milestone moments.

They all feel the same. A crippling moment of grief that takes me out of regular existence. They grip me tight but then slowly let go until next time.

During our time in Washington, we have had visitors from all walks of life—our parents, siblings, old friends, and Benji's family.

I have grown to love the visits, as they provide intimate, special times we would not get if we lived close.

When friends make the trek up to Washington to see my new life, they are hesitant and nervous. They know stepping foot in my new life is just another painstaking moment of solidifying the loss, even many years later.

The love and acceptance Benji's family and friends have for my new husband and family is breathtaking. I know the giant mountains of resentment and hurt they had to scale was more than they could bear. But God. God moved in their hearts. Moved in our hearts. Love, forgiveness, and challenging conversations brought all of us to where we are today. We still hurt, but we have all learned to hurt together.

David's family has naturally and beautifully adopted my boys and me into the Vegh family. They love my boys, remember their birthdays, and call to see how they are doing. We gained a massive blessing when I married David. We now have a third family to call home, and I know God hand-picked them to help us heal.

The legacy of Benji's favorite movies still lives epically in our home. We have seen all the new Star Wars movies with him in mind. We have watched all the recent Marvel movies, wishing he was sitting with us. We always talk about what he would have liked or how he would have critiqued it. I have shed many tears in those dark theaters with the boulder of grief squished next to me in the reclining chair. The music, the characters, the legendary endings. The cheering, the clapping at the end in honor of him.

As September rears its head each year, I don't know how

I will handle it. We have the anniversary of death layered with Jonah's birthday and Benji and I's wedding anniversary, all piled on each other in what sometimes feels like a cruel irony. I am often reminded having them all at the same time is a blessing. Just once a year, I get to grieve hard and, at the same time, celebrate the life of my firstborn son. God's symphony of life creates a beautiful mix of joy and sorrow.

Some years are smoother than others. Some years, I ease through with minimal tears; others, I am face down on the floor, earbuds in, listening to all the songs that remind me of Benji. Sometimes, I sense the need to dive head-first into all the feels. The music is like a time machine transporting me back to 2013. These moments of acknowledgment bring deep healing, although they are painful.

Over the last decade, I have experienced significant physical grief. I have felt grief take a toll on my body with debilitating anxiety, fear, and panic attacks that have landed me in the E.R. I have worked through body pains, nausea, sleeplessness, and depression. I have been through seasons of sickness that left all the doctors in Gig Harbor stumped. In 2019, I had to come to terms with the fact I wasn't sick; I was still grieving. It took a lot of soul-searching and challenging conversations with God to understand our minds and bodies are connected in intricate and delicate ways. I didn't want to believe so many years later I was still experiencing grief so profoundly. I have held epic pity parties over the years that lasted weeks and months.

Ultimately, all I experienced was the undoing of life with Benji. I was married to him for thirteen years. Perhaps it truly will take me thirteen years to live a life of grief symptom-free. I don't know what God has for me in all that, but I trust He is right here with me, holding my broken heart.

In the summer of 2021, I finally graduated from Southern New Hampshire University with my Bachelor's Degree in Creative Writing and English. It was a long five years of taking classes when I could and forging through the baby days and mountains of responsibility as a mother of four. It was a giant accomplishment that gave me the credibility to jump into the publishing world. It took me about one year of praying and searching, and in October 2022, I found a publisher and began writing.

In May 2023, I could finally take the long-awaited trip to Europe that Benji and I, along with Scott and Kami, had been planning in 2006 until I found out I was pregnant with Jonah. It was a sweet trip. Since David, Scott, Benji, and I were all in high school together, and Kami and I have been friends for twenty years, our friendships have been deep. Even though Benji wasn't there with us, we could sense him there as we laughed and remembered everything we loved about him. Before we left, I was praying with a dear friend who encouraged me that the time to live in grief is coming to an end. God has a bright, beautiful world of color waiting for me. When I was in Italy, I saw it come alive. I lived and laughed and remembered all the ways God has been faithful over the last decade of my life. It was a perfect bookend to a decade of grief.

In Malachi 3:3, we read, "He will sit as a refiner and purifier of silver, and he will purify the sons of Levi and refine them like gold and silver, and they will bring offerings in righteousness to the Lord" (ESV).

In the Ancient Near East, the refiner worked hard to purify metal with intense heat. During refining, the impurities would rise to the top to be skimmed off and thrown away. When the refiner could see his reflection in the metal, he knew the metal was thoroughly purified.

Like the refiner, God uses hard things in our lives to purify us. To refine us. He does not waste hardship or struggle. He wants to use everything we go through to refine us and to reflect Jesus.

It feels like intense heat as I trudge through, pulling off my old skin of Benji's wife to reflect who I am as Heidi, Daughter of God. I think of the pressure of the flames as they scorch my old way of thinking and living. I am and will always process my life through the lens of grief, allowing it to shape me into a new form of myself, a new self that knows God in the most intimate and personal way. A new self that can trust God with anything because He has proven himself faithful repeatedly. This is not to say I still don't fight against fear. When fear creeps in and tries to steal my joy, I am reminded, "For God has not given us a spirit of fear, but of power and of love and of a sound mind" (2 Timothy 1:7, NKJV).

God is using the process of sanctification through suffering to reveal to me who He is and the power of His strength and might (Ephesians 6:10). He has instilled in me the bravery and courage to face all the new challenges as I forge ahead in my new life.

I am constantly being stripped of all I have ever known in how to process my world. I am now forced to process this bizarre new existence with God fully.

I woke up on September 7th, 2023, but lay with my eyes closed. I realized if I had opened them and begun living, I would have lived a solid ten years without Benji's voice, laugh, and wit. I slowly opened them and saw the soft sunlight streaming through the wind-blown curtain. I sat up and swung my stone-heavy legs over the bed. I felt the weight as I pulled myself to stand. Would my first steps into a decade feel like quicksand, or could I ease my way through this day? I remembered the first steps I took away from his lifeless body ten years earlier and acknowledged the millions of steps I have now taken without him. But I felt a sense of empowerment. I sensed goodness and a deep understanding of thankfulness.

I sat in front of my large picture window with the vast evergreens in view, hot tea in hand, without a familiar sense of doom that usually accompanies this day. I sensed a deep gratitude I survived a decade of loss.

In those early days, I was forced to move forward in those first steps because my lungs didn't stop moving. My God-infused bravery pulled me across the hospital room, out into sun-drenched life, moving my lungs up and down daily for 3,650 days.

God created us to live in the confines of time. We can only

grasp a concept of existence with these boundaries. However, at this moment, I felt timeless. Time felt fluid as my mind jumped from that fall day so many years before, and I could feel a disconnect for the first time. I was out of the confines of that loss. So much life had been lived it felt like a different existence.

If I had to describe my decade of grief simply, it would be simple, maybe too simple.

I miss him. I just miss him. Over the years, he slowly melted in my heart as a husband and took residence as a friend. A friend I miss dearly every single day.

Grief, although agonizing, is the most beautiful part of my life. The deep despair has morphed into a sensation of living I have learned to appreciate. I live hard. I love hard. I feel hard. I feel more alive than I ever have. Even in my most profound moments of despair, I am grateful for all grief and loss have taught me. I would not wish this devastation on anyone, but I would wish my perspective on life for the entire world—a profound, otherworldly way of living.

I have stepped into the unknown parts of leaving this earth, as far as I could get while my heart was still beating. My grief transcends time and space and allows me to see into secret and unknown parts of our existence. I have glanced into heaven. I am thrilled to keep living and see the goodness of God continue to thrive in my life, while also longing for the day I greet Benji on the streets of gold. I will have so much to tell him about the bravery God gave me to see God's goodness in a life without him.

Acknowledgments

To Benji: What I wouldn't give to tell you all of these things. I imagine sitting down with you and reading this book to you. The list of things to tell you is a million miles long and keeps growing. This book barely touches the surface. Thank you for loving me. Thank you for comforting me in my pain before you left. Thank you for blessing me and helping me continue living and finding new love. Thank you for loving me and living life with me for sixteen beautiful years. Losing you was beyond excruciating, but I would do it all again for you to be healed. Even though saying goodbye tore out my heart, I am at peace knowing you are no longer suffering. You would be astonished at our perfect little boys. They have grown into strong young men, and you are stamped all over who they are. We miss you!

To David: Thank you for coming into my life and deciding to stay, although it was messy. Thank you for loving me and my boys so genuinely and beautifully. I thank God he brought us together and brought beauty out of our dark circumstances. Being your wife and parenting our blended family with you is my greatest joy. I can't wait to watch our children grow together and spend the rest of my life with you. I love you!

To Jonah: My first baby. I am sorry we had to go through something so tragic. It tore me apart to see you lose your daddy, but I see it has made you stronger and shaped you into who you are today. I pray you can look back at your life and see how God took care of us and brought so many people into our lives to help us heal. Always remember I love you, and you have a God who created you, loves you, and has big things for you. He will use our story for His good. I love you, Jonah.

To Isaac: You are my silly boy. I love you so much and can't wait to see what God has for you. We experienced significant loss together, but God used it for good. Seeing you lose your daddy was my biggest heartbreak, but you are stronger for it, Isaac. You are uniquely made, and God has big plans for you. Remember that no matter what you go through in life, God is with you, loves you, and has a purpose for all things. I love you, Isaac.

To Harlo: Thank you for making me a stepmom. I feel blessed to have you in my life. It has been a joy to watch you grow, and I can't wait to see where God takes you. Thank you for being part of our blessings from our loss! I love you!

To Emmy: You are my most precious gift from loss. You were so wanted and loved, my sweet girl. I was broken, and God used your life to bless me and your daddy. Benji always wanted me to have a daughter, and I have one in you. God has great things for you in your life. I can't wait to see how God uses your spunky personality to change the world! I love you!

To my family: Thank you for being my solid rock when Benji died. You all showed up for me in so many tangible ways. I was broken, hurting, and unable to care for myself well, and you all stepped in and filled in the gaps. Thank you for supporting me when it was hard to see me move forward in my life. Thank you for sending us to Washington with love, although it was hard to see us go. Thank you for loving me and my family and being there for us when we needed you the most.

To Benji's Family: We did it. We have lived over a decade without our sweet Benji. It was hard to see division in our family as I strived to continue living. I know it is hard to see me in a new life, but thank you for ultimately moving past the uncomfortable pain and accepting our new path. You are all deeply special to me, and I am thankful that we have landed in a good place in our relationships; we will always be family. I am forever grateful that we took Benji's advice to always be excellent to one another.

To The Vegh Family: When the boys and I lost Benji, it was hard to imagine a future without him. When David and Harlo came into our lives, we gained a bonus family in all of you. I know that it was difficult for you to swallow David marrying a widowed mother, but you extended grace and embraced the three of us as your own. Thank you for loving us so sincerely. Thank you for welcoming us into your family and celebrating our life with us. You are all tangible proof of God's goodness.

To Benji's Friends: Thank you for showing up in the darkest days of my life. Thank you for loving my boys and doing what you could do for us, even with broken hearts. If you have any feelings of guilt, please give yourself grace. Benji put an enormous responsibility on your shoulders, not knowing how excruciating it would be. There is no room for hard hearts, and I genuinely hope and pray you are finding healing in your giant loss.

To Capital Church: Thank you for being our safe place during Benji's sickness and into my grief. You showed up for me in so many ways. Thank you for supporting the boys and me. Thank you for helping us celebrate such a beautiful life lived in Benji. I am forever grateful for your place in our life.

To the healthcare workers: Thank you for the incredible and intentional care you gave to Benji during his treatment and last days. I was unable to fully advocate for him, and I felt you helped me make the right decisions at the right times. Thank you to the hospice workers who not only took care of Benji but also took care of my boys as you blessed them with a trip to Comicon. You were all a blessing on the hardest days.

To Kelci and Tyler: Thank you for helping us form a beautiful blended family life with grace and ease. Although unconventional, you are family to us, and we are blessed to have you in our lives. Kelci, I never thought I would gain a best friend when I married David, but God does big, awesome things!

A Hard Journey to the Good

To our Washington friends: There are no words to describe the blessing you have all been since our time in Washington. To our neighborhood village, who help us raise our kids; to our church friends, who have helped me walk through dark grief days and who talk of Benji as if he is an old friend; and to all the other people who have crossed our paths and made Washington our home, thank you for loving our family!

Bibliography

1. Lewis, C.S. *Mere Christianity.* San Francisco: Harper, 2021.

2. Eliott, Elisabeth. *Passion and Purity.* Michigan: Revell Publishing, 2013.

3. Voskamp, Ann. *One Thousand Gifts.* Thomas Nelson, 2012.

4. Gibson, Mel dir. *Braveheart* USA:Paramount Pictures, 1995.

5. Eliott, Elisabeth

6. Egar, Edith. *The Choice.* New York, New York: Scribner, 2018.

7. Sonnenfeld, Barry, director. *Men In Black.* Columbia Pictures, Sony Pictures Releasing, 1997. 1h 38m. Hulu.

8. A Great Big World. "Say Something." 2014, Spotify.

9. Keller, Timothy, and Kathy Keller. *The meaning of marriage: Facing the complexities of commitment with the wisdom of god.* Penguin Books, 2016.

10. Milne, A. A., & Shepard, E. H. *The Complete Tales of Winnie-the-Pooh.* Dutton Children's Books, 2016.

11. Lewis. C.S. *The Problem of Pain.* San Francisco: Harper One, 2015.

About Heidi...

Heidi Vegh is a creative writer and widow with a passion for sharing her story of loss and new life. She is a remarried mother of four, navigating the blended family life after the loss of her first husband to cancer in 2013. She longs to use her writing as a way to encourageothers who have experienced loss, and guide them on the road to healing. She contributes to her blog found at www.mrsheidivegh.com, sharing stories and devotionals of faith stemming from her loss and healing, mothering, and her blended and complex family. She graduated from Southern New Hampshire University with a degree in Creative Writing and English. Heidi has a heart for sharing Jesus with women and encouraging them in their faith walk. When she is not writing, she loves to travel and adventure with her family. She lives in the small coastal town of Gig Harbor, Washington, where she loves to visit her local coffee shops and sip on a matcha latte while she writes.Visit her Facebook and Instagram (@mrsheidivegh) to learn more.

www.ingramcontent.com/pod-product-compliance
Lightning Source LLC
Chambersburg PA
CBHW070139080526
44586CB00015B/1759